Alegmi Sofia
Publication
(Hasafa)

On **Europe** *Steps*

Happened in North Africa,
The south beach
of Mediterranean

By
Alegmi Sofia
The Libyan Author
2014

Hug

Dear readers.

Many novels translated from the author mother language, so the translator tact of his ability to choice the correct words which can be means his thinking will be prevails in the text, in other side when the author writes his work using other language does not his mother language, he will make some mistakes, and he can not be able to use the eloquent language which be suitable for the occasion or event, also he will choices his words carefully because he does not knows the used and the unused words, in other way author repeats some words because he think maybe the reader had not known what he meant, which lessens the reader comfort, but anyway many people like the author original text with any possible shorts.

Therefore, please use your imagination to be close of me in every details, do not forget that I will indicate to events want you know what I want to say to you deeply, and forgive me for any mistake.

With my best regards

Alegmi Sofia

(1)
Satan partners

Miss. Maria is a Milanian (Italian) lady, forty years old, has a beauty trace on her face was not enough to get husband, she was engaged three times but her relations cut before ten years, then none wanted her after, Maria was a religious person, she has been going to church every Sunday, and participated the church with many religion culture meetings and care efforts in Italy.

Since ten years when she lost hope to get marriage, Maria looking was as an ascetic lady, wears her dresses however, lonely, away of her neighbors and friends, she has been not talking everybody, few times along years she looked in nice or sexy dresses went to certain place, then shortly she returned back to close her door again for many days.

Maria have not a shame acts, limited her going out to market, bank, and church, Maria has two secretes shame things she did time to time, wanted forgot after done, time to time she has been spying on her neighbors sex doing, or watching forbidden movies and TV channels, therefore sleeps naked enjoys herself with some special tools she bought them to not looking for men anymore.

Maria has a narrow religion view, wasn't had a large culture could helped her to know facts in large view, she has inherited a big stubbornness from her mother, she has been worrying when her sister decided *to married a Muslim Youngman met her in Rome before long time ago, she stood in the way of her sister marriage for long months with her mother, but her sister with her father were went on, but she did not felt that she is a member of his sister family as an ant, she hated her sister husband and his sons, just because they are not Christians, she looks them as enemies of Christ, also that marriage made a hidden wall limited the relation with her sister and her family, after her parent death and her sister been in Libya, Maria became lives alone in her parent house which become old and derby, it was a small house has three rooms and small poor garden, in old quarter in Milan, Maria used her old parent bedroom to be her bedroom, she doesn't cares about house cleanness or furniture arrangement, her house always in anarchy, passing her parent little monthly death benefit money for his life needs and saves some for any future emergency.*

Her sister Sozan became a wife to a small Libyan trader, since twenty three years ago, named Mahmoud Bera, since Marriage they have been living in owned small nice house in Tripoli south environ with them three adult sons, Mourad, Ali, and them daughter Salma.

Bera family were respected from them known people, Mr. Mahmoud and his wife a nice simply life partners, and them sons were followed on them parents, every thing was in fine side, nothing lead to worry, Mahmoud works in his food shop earning good profits let them family in good money position, they have every necessary needs and more.

Maria had never visited her sister family before, in fact she never crossed the Mediterranean to south, her sister invited here to visit her family in Tripoli many times, but Maria she didn't, she has a foggy look to the south Mediterranean Muslims rudder, she had satisfied with her sister and family visits to Italy time to time while them parents were in life, after them parents death her sister Sozan visits became few and short, she was lonely in her parent house in Milan, missed her older sister.

When Sozan has not been visiting Milan for couple years, she sent a new official invitation in the summer of 2010 beginning to her sister Maria to spend some time with her family in Tripoli, Maria felt that she is longing for her sister Sozan, that feeling encouraged her to comply her sister invitation, but her longing mixed with some scare and unknown worry, her previous information about Arabs and Muslims let someone religious like her been in unbalance feeling status.

Maria was has lonely friend was a butcher, in her house lane corner, called Maurice, he was an educated man inherited a small butchery from his dead father before tens of year, cines that time hi have been working in them meat-shop, Maria bought her weekly meat need from him since many years ago, time by time became friends, he looked like a small philosopher in butcher dress, Maria always discussing with him time to time many stand in the way problems, Maurice always has good and clever ideas for many subjects, also his funny character let his clients and friends approved for him, he was married, had two sons, but he made sex with Maria many times in her dead parent house, in the beginning of them relation, but always they have been looking them selves as a friends not as a lovers

Maria decided to talk with Maurice about her trip to visit her sister in Tripoli and her worry thinks, she wants know Maurice viewpoint about her obsession about Muslims, Arabs and Libya, then she went to him at guessed free work time to talk, Maurice laughed at Maria when she told him her information about Libyans and Arabs at generally, he charged her with insanity, she surprised, she never listened that Muslims or Arabians are a people, like every people in the world, and they are humans as other humans in generally, and if there is someone bad, is every people have bad and good, and there is not special worry about them, he advised her to looks every people as one, as person, everybody of them has mother, father, sisters, brothers, neighbors, friend, because he is a human-being, insure there is some viewpoints here or there, but the international communications lessen the dissimilarity between peoples globally, now, everybody is as others, the religions are make some difference life viewpoints, but human been viewpoints became better than few tens years ago, he had spoken as a teacher gives a lesson for stupid student, with sarcastic dialect, that act embarrassed her feeling, she had been never saw him like today, he wasn't been nicely with her, seemed like someone fed-up with his stupid friend, his talk made her in perplexity, but when he indicated her as someone lives out of time she decided that she had ought to go without debate.

she left out her friend shop with more worry and misunderstanding.

She hided her angry wave which mobilized her chest and weighted her heart, she was worried and now after his friend visiting became nerve and impatient to know the truth, she did not understood many of her friend suddenly talk, she repented of her last visiting to Maurice, who talked all that nonsense, Arabians and Muslims never had been as every worldwide people, they are stupid, idolaters, and dirty, never she understood how her beautiful sister married with one of them?, and how she still in life in that barbarian countries?, never she imagined herself in same position, her sister was crazy!, how she assented to marry someone idolater, one of the Jesus enemy ?, The Satan partner, and her best friend raved that drivel talk as an evil philosopher, which make someone like her prefer to be in death before hearing that cheat.

Muslims were in down people, had not been like others, and never will be like others, she hated them since her younger was, they were our enemies from history beginning been, the history never lies, she is talking herself time to time during few days later when she remember her sister invitation.

She cut the phone connections when she hear her sister voice comes from Tripoli, she knew that she will encourage her to come, before few days she was listening to her and exchange salutes and chat, but after Maurice last visiting she became confused, she was thinking and repeating the last Maurice laughing talk time to time, which made her as a drunk been, she changed her way to avert passing in the way of Maurice meat-shop, she don't want see him anymore, she guessed that he is a Muslim in secret, one of the Satan partners.

On Sunday, through her weekly church visit, Maria decided to meet The nun of church called Miss. Bella Be, who has some special consent with her, the nun was as her friend, talked with here many times in deep and touched that she was a good Christ religious cultured, so she can tell her the truth, after prayer they met each other separated in one of an empty church rooms, as what Maria wanted, after short time, Maria told the nun with regret:

- Dear sister, with my apology, I have a sister married with a Muslim person before long time, lives in Tripoli with her adult sons, she wants me visit her for few months, but as you know that Tripoli is the capital of Libya in North Africa, it is a Muslims country, I hate Muslims and I don't want go there, but I longing to my sister, can you give me an advices to do the right?.

Eyes of nun were widened, filled by astonishment and scare, but she controlled herself quickly and replay Maria with soft voice:

- Oh dear!, you have the right to apology, your sister was a shameful, oh god!, how Christian lady is believer in Jesus can marry his enemy, idolater one, and lade his seeds in her womb to give Satan a new soldier to fight Jesus?.

Nun said that words and went in short prayer with closed eyes, Maria felt that her soul came back again to her body, and her think regulated again, she felt that she was became good, as some heavy load *took away from her shoulder, sat in her chair waiting nun prayer finishing, after few minutes nun open her eyes and smiled in her face and told her softly as someone talking himself:*

-Ok, dear, do not worry, comeback to me tomorrow and I will tell you what do you must do!, She said that and stood up ended that short meeting.

In return way, Maria was happy and pleasures, her mind eased, tomorrow her nun sister will tell her the solution of her trouble, a faithfully solution, not that Maurice evil chitchat.

The day after, Maria was home, she has felt that she don't want see anybody in this day, wants be alone, spent all the day time between bed, kitchen, bathroom.

At ten o clock morning of the next day Maria surprised when she heard her door been knocked, there is someone on the door step informed her to meet Ms. Bella in church now, he said that and returned back to his coming way, Maria hurried to church, she found Miss Bella in her reception with an unknown man, separately in the same next meeting room, Miss. Bella hailed Maria with large smile and apologized to her about her suddenly invitation, and requested her to sit-down on large chair and relax, after Maria sat, Miss. Bella introduced the unknown man to Maria as her friend George, an immigration officer, who consulted him about her future trip to Tripoli.

Mr. George proceeded to Maria with an extended hand, he shook her hand with some hardness, with large welcomes smile, then Bella and George took chairs apposite her, after few exchanged smiles, Miss.

Bella started talking with full attention to Maria, used a soft voice mixed with a large encouragement smile:
- Ok .. dear, I sent a man to your house to invite you today because you were forgot to came back to me yesterday as what I advised you the day before, and Mr. George wished know you as one of the sincere Jesus believers will go to infidel land, that is why I sent to you in hurry.

She said that with carefully looking to Maria's face, when she felt that Maria be reassured to her, she continues:
- As you said before that the Muslims, Arabians, were the Jesus enemies have been abiding in all Middle east and all north Africa, then when some one like you go there. he must didn't forget his lord Jesus, he must use his effort to change the realty to his lord benefit by any way, if you are really one of Jesus soldiers, faithfully and honest as what we know in this church then so you are able to do something as your possible in Muslims land!.

That talking did her conglomerated in her sitting on the chair, she said with a low shamed voice, looking down, as someone guilty wanted to say the truth:
- Ok, but how I can serve my lord in Muslims land?.

Mr. George does noted her confused and shame been, he knew by his experience the Maria character, she is simple and spontaneously, this kind of people needs time to understand everything new, he draws a big smile and say to Maria:
- Dear Maria, We are here to help you not to confusing you, You are the best one of the church parish, Ms. Bella wants your easy help for the god not for herself,

if you can do it that is good, if you do not, then no problem, you can do what do you want!.

George peaceful words made Maria self re-backed to calm, then Maria began understand what they were talked about. but not clearly, The nun saw her wavering, so she told her with calm voice:

- As Mr. George said We are here to help you, if you can distribute some of Gospel Arabic copies in secret and invite people to Christ, that is an easy way to serve your lord in Muslims land.

Maria felt a great happiness feeling, she felt that she is an important person, can do something for her lord, easy and effective, but she broke down again when she think about something, so she looked to them together and said:

- But how I can do that?, the Libyan airport customs will find them in her baggage!.

George told here with encourage voice:

- don't worry about that, we will carry it to you to your sister home step in Tripoli, just we need your secret effort to be one of the lord Jesus soldier in Libya.

The meeting condition became clear and comfortable, every body were happy, that meeting spent five hours talked about many deep details through many drink and fast food, and continued few next days in the church to learning Maria how she can be a good soldier of Jesus in Muslim land, with some advices about her secret movements in Tripoli when she become alone among Muslim people, and charged her by hatred for everything and everybody not Christian, or European.

Maurice guessed that his friend Maria was angry because of him, so after some days later after her last visiting went to her house after his butchery close time carried some fresh meat in small sac in his hand as a present for her, he knocked her home door few time before Maria opened it, she surprised when she saw Maurice on her door steps, she stood in the open door space looking for him without any welcoming, he smiled for her and handed her the small sac, but she still stood without movement, just looking to him with death eyes on stony face, Maurice return back his hand beside his body and told her with laugh:

- What?.. do you became insane?.

But Maria did not said anything, then he continued with more laughing voice:

- Did you forgot talk?, or forgot me?.

Maria asked him with hard voice:

- Are you a Muslim?.

The question surprised Maurice, but he still smiled and laugh, then hi told her by his academic voice accent:

- Do you know what is word (Insane) means in Arabic language?.

But Maria did not replied, she still standing up as statue, then Maurice continued:

- (Insane)means in Arabic language (Human), so every human has some (Insane) in his mind, now you are in insane status!.

He said that and guffawed in higher, that act made Maria in nerve, her face became redden, then she said by high angry voice:

- You are a Muslim in secret!, You are an enemy of Jesus, an agent to Arabians, Satan partner!.

She said that and shut-up her door with hard on Maurice face, Maurice screamed behind the door with nerves voice:

- You have to go to mind-sanatorium not to Libya!.

He said that and returned back to his home with lost smiles.

———

(2)
Create your Luck!

Azza and Faris Hani were adults beautiful twins, living with them mother in nice small home been near Bera family, them father was died before few years ago, Azza is a teacher in nearly intermediate school, Faris finished his high school two years ago, he is waiting his turn to hire, thousands of young-men as Faris waiting since many years to be in some government place, as an official employee, or however, them mother named Fatma became not in good health and mood after her husband death, she was beautiful happy lady, but now she doesn't care about her beauty or looking, she seem as some one grew up many years suddenly.

Hani family income was Azza salary and them father Monthly death-hood was giving to his widow, month by month since them father death..

Faris was a religious Youngman, incline to religious extremism, is a friend of Beras sons, in spite of them characters difference, Mourad and his brother Ali were a regulated Young-men, but they spend time together when they have time.

Azza is in difference with her brother and her mother too, she is a liberalist person, loves the life enjoyment without limitations, she is a friend of Salma Bera too.

In the last corner of the quarter main road there is a very beautiful house abode by Barnous family,

Barnouss was a suspicious family, multiply suspicious talking been around them life and behaviors, Mr. Fathi Barnous, the father was a pimp for his beautiful wife Najat and daughters Mouna and Ferdous, always Barnouss make noisy evening parties in them house receiving many rich people coming anywhere from, his son Fouzi was in prison for two years ago, he was a druggist, use and trade drugs, the court judgment was ten years prison for him, but his father try to seduce someone by her daughters and wife who is able to make his son been in freedom again.

On the quarter south far side there is a small Christ church managed by some unknown foreign people, opened its large doors in Sundays for Christians who coming to prayer.

Bera family fell in deep happy when them aunt Maria informed them that she will be in Tripoli after few days to spend some months with them, specially her sister Souzan was too happy, but Maria did not gave them the correct time of her arrive, as her unknown actions doing usually, Maria haughty complex prevented her to gave her sure appointment arrive to her sister family to waiting her in Tripoli airport, her sister try to phone her but she did not replied, then the family were in open time waiting.

In the airplane to Tripoli, Maria chair was beside an electrical French Youngman, seemed as a nice gentleman, after few time of the airplane take-off Maria wanted to know him, she presented herself to him using her little English language when she knew that her setting neighbor is a French man, hi welcomed her and presented himself with too slowly

English words when he felt that her English language is too little, and he don't speak Italian, after that, they exchanged some of them general personal information, but Maria surprised the Youngman when she asked him with nerves:

- Sir, I want know how gentleman like you work with Jesus enemies?.

The Youngman amazed to her asking, but he controlled his amazement and asked her with perplexity:

- Who are they Jesus enemies?.

Maria smiled for his stupid mind (as her seemed) and continued:

-The Libyans, Arabs, Muslims, all of them are Jesus enemies!.

The Youngman guessed that Maria has been joking with him, then he laughed and said as someone talk to himself surely:

- Oh. Dear, Libyans are very nice people often, I am working with them since five years in happiness, I have many Libyans and Arabians friends.

Maria never Imagined that this gentleman could said that trash words, Satan became been everywhere, suddenly extended her neck and turned her head to searching for an empty place, when she saw some of empty places in the airplane back, she stood up and changed her place to one of the empty places, like someone runaway from death, that act generated a noise in the airplane silent, that act made some curious passengers inquired for happen, while that French man in unbelievable to what was she did, but he still in his place smiles as crazy one on faces of passengers who turned to him.

A Swiss trader passenger who has more attention left his chair and sat beside the French Youngman and asked him about what happened, the Youngman told him everything about the Italian passenger Maria, and her nervous, the Swiss man patted on the Youngman shoulder and went back to Maria new setting, he bent his body on her chair and whispered in her ear with soft voice:

- I had been admired to you, You are not lonely who respect Jesus in this world, contact me in Tripoli I will be happy to meet you, please contact me in any time when you need a friend like you!.

He said that and gave her his visit-card which contain his name Mr. Bernard Shome and his contacts information in Tripoli and Swiss.

In the Tripoli airport she did not found any difficulty, then after short time she was on the front of the airport with her luggage and presents to her sister searching for a taxi.

By her good or bad luck the taxi driver was a Libyan man speaks the Italian language well, Maria was happy that she found someone native speak Italian, even hi is one of his lord enemies, Maria gave the address of her sister's house to the taxi driver who gave her his visit-card to contact him when she need a taxi to go anywhere, The taxi driver named Mohamed Lamin, Maria spit in secret when she read her name in his visit-card which she took.

Bera family welcomed the aunt Maria, Mahmoud closed his shop and return back to his home to be one of his family who welcoming his darling wife sister, Maria get a nice bedroom waiting for her, she surprised when she saw her sister home, it was large and modern, everything was cleaned and perfect, her room was large with remote-control curtain, a special bathroom, TV, computer connected with internet and phone, and special air-condition, oh god, she couldn't believed that her sister lives in comfort life, her sons and husband welcoming gave her love and longing she has not a place to receive it, when she was lonely in her special bedroom to take some rest, she felt herself is in deep eddy without end made herself fall in sleep.

In supper, Maria amazed when she saw that her sister family made a special welcoming party for her, the close Mahmoud neighbors: Said a barber, Saleh a mechanic, Massoud a baker, Bechir an electric engineer and Ali a civil engineer carried their ladies for supper welcome party, and some of Mahmoud neighbors and friends came too, for that there were many ladies around the table seem beautiful and educated came to share her sister welcoming to her sister, they treated her as a lost sister came back after long time, Souzan translated to Maria every words of the ladies talking, Mahmoud took his diner with his two sons in other place to give a large personal space to ladies to be relax and easy, it is a good act he was did, Salma was nice, looking to her aunt with love eyes, Maria found herself in a family relationship condition moved something in herself deep she thought it was lost, she lived her last ten years alone, without friends or anybody care her or has any really love to her, for that she left the welcome party and went to her room to cry as a little girl.

Maria forgot her hate temporary, her premature information about Arabs and Muslims who were in her seem as Jesus enemies, she forgot all that as a child forgot her return way in crammed carnival, everything was as not really, she think that his sister lives in miserable life with stupid and dirty family, among barbarian neighbors, she think that her sister have been here causes of her sons, Arabians are not as what she was thought, they are humans as what Maurice try to inform her,.. oh, Maurice that vile one, but she find a short in Mr. George information gave to her who is an immigration officer knows everything about Arabians, he told her that they are stupid, dirty, barbarian people, but from the airport up to now she found everything is normally and organized.

Souzan followed Maria to her room, when she found her sister is crying, she hugged her and cried with her too, Maria felt her sister hug as cold water extinguished her soul and mind fire, a familiar feeling lost since long time, for that those two sisters fell in deep cry, and they felt a soft hands held both of them and cry with, she was Salma cried for them crying.

After few minutes Souzan cleaned her eyes and left room to care her guests, while Salma and her aunt spent some time in long hug, and set down on the large bed exchanging smiles and love looks with wet eyes, a few minutes later, Salma and her aunt joined the party people with large smiles and more courage.

The day next, after breakfast Sozan informed her sister Maria about some of Arabian reception habits, which means that every neighbors will invite her to them homes for lunch or supper, and they will present her some presents, in them homes they will exchange with her some personal information to know her well, and in the future she will be a part of them families.

The Arabians reception habits astonished Maria, she blamed herself for her stupid, she did not remember at ones that she asked her sister for anything about Arabians and them habits, she was never discussed her sister about her life?, her think?, her relations?, what is Arabians think?, what is Islam?, what is the difference between Islam and Christ?, how Muslims look to Christians?.

Now she become as a blinded person, has some old dark information grew-up through unaware years without any discuss, why she did not asked her sister about every thing before long time?, why when her sister came to Milan with her family form many years did not spent some time with them for knew each other?, her sister daughter cried for her?, even she did not knew her aunt practically, from time to time she looked Salma without any conversation or any human relationship, she was looking them as some disturb barbarian people came to spend some time and they have to go in dark again, without regret, she was proud and haughty.

When she remembered all what was she happened she fall in silent cry on facing her lovely sympathetic old sister, Sozan hugged her sister and kissed her had and encouraged her to throw her sadness in same time of cleaning her eyes by her soft perfumed scarf.

In deep self of Maria there is one important question, she ought to asking her sister about her religion, is she still Christian or changing her religion to the Islam?, this question caused to her many worries through all the last years, but because her relation with her sister Sozan was not deeply, then she delayed her question to an future time.

Mahmoud was desirous to furnish all what Maria needs to make her in best ease, then Maria spent the few next days in home with her sister and her neighbors in full happiness.

Masjed (Mosque) Imam saw Azza Hani and Salma Bera together had walking in Market with both of Barnouss daughters Najat and Ferdous, they had exchanging laughs and jokes with high noise, then he informed whole of Mahmoud father of Salma, and Mr. Faris the brother of Azza, the two men became angry.

*Mahmoud delayed his angry to his home back return time, But Faris went directly to his mother to inform her, Ms. Fatma became angry too, but she ordered her son to not talk with her sister about, she wished to talk with her daughter alone, when Azza came back from her work found her mother wasn't in usually behavior with her, she tried to know what was happened, but her mother waiting her to be in relax to inform her, after lunch when Azza went to her room Fatma followed her and sat-down in her front on the bed, this conversation rotated between them, Mother firstly told her daughter with full of her angry voice:
-Do you wants make me crazy?*

Azza surprised but she smiled on her mother face and replied her with relax voice:

- What was happened?, why you are angry?, I met Faris in my return way but he did not looked or talk to me?.

- You are a teacher .. an educated person .. how you had a friendship with Barnouss? .. are you crazy? .. or you wants make me and you respected brother crazy too?.

Azza laughs with high voice and said:

- Oh, so .. that rascal Masjed Imam betrayed to you and Faris what did he saw! .. oh, that stupid did not let me alone .. I and Salma saw him in the market, and we knew that he saw us .. one day I will kill him .. that stupid person.

- The Masjed Imam looking for your reputation, he know that you and Salma are a good people, sons of good families, so he didn't wanted everybody see you or Salma with whores exchanging jokes with high voices on faces of everybody who knew them reality!.

- Whores or not whores that is them business .. I and Salma looking to them as a neighbors .. so there is nothing stands in way of our friendship ... that is not a shame when neighbors were been together .. I will not let that stupid Imam steals my freedom!.

Her mother feeling hurt, always her daughter seemed to her as an unknown one, did not care about anything but her self, angry wave trembled her body:

- Since your born, you have been selfish and stubborn, everybody respecting us because we are a respected family, you and me are not whores, your brother is a gentleman, you will put our heads down when you care just for you self, and your false freedom, I have been regretting that your evil more than your good, selfish

and rash, look .. my last words is .. if you don't correct your behavior, and cut any relation with everybody not good or respected, so I have other way with you!.

She said that and left the room with angry and slapped the door with full force echoed in silent home.

Azza did not be angry, all her life was not accorded with her mother and brother, she looking to them as believers for an antique thinking but she esteemed her self is a modern person, have to live her life with freedom, wants try to do and test everything without any limitation, for that in secret behind of her mother and brother attention, she has been trying to do every thing as possible as soon, even that forbidden doing, she running to not let any moment passing without any enjoyment, she was as an enjoyment crazy, her family did not knew many of her secret acts, she met the both Barnous daughters many times in secret who learned her many forbidden doings, after that, step by step, she brought her friend Salma Bera to one of them secret sexual meetings, but Salma was more than Azza carefully and care, she hated any forbidden things which the girls done, Azza can be in normal relation with Salma, but with Barnouss is too difficult, all people around her refused any kind of relation with them at all. Azza Loved Salma as a good friend can reach her in anytime but she need her for other things which she hated and refused, but some times she kissed her lips suddenly, or rest in her hold for some time.

Azza phoned Salma to comes to her home, they closed the door as what the did when they were alone, Azza informed her girlfriend about all the conversation with her mother done, Salma has been worry because she guessed the Masjed Imam was informed her father too, then he will make a trouble to her, her aunt been in home will complicate the problem, she don't want her aunt listening her father scolding.

At night, after Mahmoud home return he been alone with his wife and informed her all what Masjed Imam said and ask for her to talk with Salma to cut her relation with the Barnouss, all of them and every bad person, his wife been worry too, but she smiled to reassured him, after that she went to her daughter and transferred all what her father said and order, Salma did not discussed her mother, she agreed all the talking without any objection, just to limit the problem, as possible, out of her aunt hearing.

A few days later, Maria knew many things about her sister life, and what it is happening around her, she did not forgot her godly mission, but she re-organizing her ideas, Muslims not as what she have been informed, some times she suspected her self in Milan, there is no difference, Arabians like Italians, so she must change her plan, but before that, she must ask her sister to know her position, if she is still Christian, then she must help her, but if she became a Muslim so she must be careful with her movement.

In one night Maria was lonely with her sister talked about them memories in Milan when they were been young, they laughed sometimes and regretted other times, suddenly Maria asked her sister:
- Did you still Christian Sozan?
Sozan did not surprised, she smiled and replied her sister seriously:
- No dear, I am a Muslim since I married Mahmoud!.

Maria said:- I am sorry that you left your parent religion!.

Sozan made large smile and said carefully:
- There no sorry, Islam like Christ, everything same, everything forbidden in Christ is forbidden in Islam, all of them are worshipping the same god (Allah).
Maria: - If there is same, so why you left Christ, our parent religion?.
- Darling ,They are same, but Islam has more than details!, Muslims believe in Christ too!.
Maria surprised:
-What did you say?, do Muslims believe in Christ?.
Sozan smiled and replied:
- Yes darling, every Muslim must believes to Christ!.
- How?.
- Muslims believe in all God Prophets, and them books, Muslims did not forced anybody to be Muslim, for that you see many Christians in Muslims land, eight percent of Egyptians are Christians, and every Arabian Countries has Christians have churches and everything.

Maria have been in unbalance status again, Arabs not barbarian, they have a culture, she didn't listened her sister when she wished to her a good night and left the room, she still in her place for long time stonily turning the new information in her mind with silence.

Day next, Salma asked her mother to invite Azza to sleep with her because she is lonely and want her friend to be with her, Sozan agreed her daughter request with pleasure, then afternoon Azza came to Mahmoud home, the two girls spent some time in

Salma room and sat-down in the TV room listening music, Maria came and sat with them, the two girls surround Maria asked her about Milan, Italy, her life there, her friends ...est.

Maria was happy for them questions, she told them many nice Italian stories, Italian marriage manners, cooking, native dance, they exchanged many jokes and laugh, she was older than them but they returned her to her young been, she laughed with them with high noise made Sozan let everything and came to share with them the funny session.

After few time the two girls danced on the tape songs, the two girls was very skilled, them young graceful bodies and dance acts was beautiful, they imitated many sexual funny acts in them dances, which made Maria loved them deeply, but everything stopped slowly when Ali and his brother Mourad entered the home back, and the silent be back in the home again.

Azza spent the night with Salma, in the morning they seemed exhausted as they not get sleep.

———————

(3)
Incredible Things

Masjed Imam after Acer (afternoon) prayer asked the prayers to listen to him, everybody in Masjed sat-down carefully, The imam sat-down apposite them and said with his sonorous voice:
- My brothers, Our quarter contains a goodness families, but there is some bad families been in our quarter spread out evil and vice acts everywhere, our families are in danger, we growing up our children to be goodness people, but our efforts will be fail if some bad people among us moved by Satan forces to backslide them, we must do something against them however been, we must fight to pull out the Satan seeds from our quarter as soon as possible or we will rue in delay time, when the regret will do nothing.
From the Masjed hall back side, some whispering been to high, then some one said with strong voice:
- Imam, This is Police jobs, Who we can drive away people out of our quarter?
Other one replied:
- The police men is them clients!
Other one said:
- Courts spend long time and need Proofs, and the evil people are cautious of any proof, they are criminals know the law more than lawyers!.
Imam Said cut all speaking:

- Please think about that, to solve this big problem, and we will talk again to find a way.. Allah helps us.

All prayers let the Masjed with noise talking in the same subject everybody of them has a viewpoint, but Imam stay in his sat asking Allah to help them.

Barnous sisters decided visiting Bera family in cause of Maria arrived welcoming, they knew that they are unwanted people, that cause made Salma has been visiting them in secret, but they want been as a normal neighbors, always they take the opportunities to make them family relation with neighbors be normal, many times they were drove out, but they did not cared, did not cut them relation with everybody, then they had coming to Beras home dressed shameful dresses as them usually behavior and knocked the door, Souzan surprised when she found them on her door step, but she controlled herself and smile on them face with amazing face, inquires to the cause of them visit, Maria came to her behind inquiring too, the two girls saluted Sozan and told her that they were came to welcoming her sister arrived Maria, Maria when heard her name dislodged her sister by carefully and handed her hand to the sisters, the sisters checked her hands with pleasure, Maria invited them to enter home, Souzan more surprised of her sister doing, she know that her sister has not any information about these two girls, but she pretended that she is welcoming them too with cold laughs and dead smiles.

Salma and Azza was in home salon playing cards, they surprised too when they saw Barnous sisters entered followed by Souzan and Maria, the two sisters were happy that they could enter Bera home, they laughed highly to Salma and Azza and hugged them deeply as they did not saw them before long time, Salma and Azza pretended too to be as they are welcoming them, they knew that Madame Souzan doing a big fault, they did not saw what Maria did in the door step.

The two sisters sat on faced of Azza and Salma, set them hands on Azza and Salma thighs as lovers doing, talking with sexy acts and bad joking, Sozan informed her sister that everything is normal and let the salon to bring some drink to her forced guests, in that Sozan bad-luck time Mahmoud came back home for an emergency something, he stopped in the door of the salon as statue did not believed his eyes, he became in full angry, but he controlled himself and run to inside searching for his wife, all of who been in salon heard his scolding to his wife about the Barnous sisters existence in them home!, Sozan tried to explain what was happened in low voice, but Mahmoud left her and came back to salon room and asked the two Barnous sisters to leave home!, they were scared looking Mahmoud angry seriously, Maria did not understood anything, she still in her settee as deaf, smiling for everybody around her. Barnouss stood-up indicated to Maria trying to explain to him that they came to shared with Maria welcoming, Maria when she saw them signs to her and heard her name repeating, stood-up and hugged the both sisters, Maria saw Mahmoud angry, seemed for her that he dismissed her guests, two nice girls came special to see and welcoming her!, Mahmoud must respect her and her guests, he insulted her, she is not a slave, she has been thinking in this wrong stream, she considered that act is an aggressive action against her, as a reaction, when they were left the home Maria followed the sisters in them way to home out as a protest against Mahmoud doing, Mahmoud followed his relative calling her to come back home but Maria went with the two sisters with laughing to them home, and Mahmoud return back with his full angry.

Barnouss welcomed Maria in them home with laughing about them funny adventure, they told them father and mother about them going to Bera house and all what was happen, the family rounded Maria with full happiness, because nobody from them neighbors has been visiting them, but this brave lady Maria did, she broke them neighbors blockade, Father and mother blessed them daughters did, Maria she saw that these people welcoming her visit but she did not understood the deep reason of them acts, that they are going to do anything to break them around relationship blockade, she look and feel them apparent acts but don't know the background of its, also nobody from Barnous family speak Italian then they signs and marks to Maria to communicate with her, but in few time later, Mr. Fathi phoned a friend who speak Italian to translate with Maria, accidentally he was the taxi driver who brought Maria from the airport, Mr. Mahmoud Lamin, that accident make Maria acclaimed for his coming, also he was in same, Barnouss did not explained to Maria the really reason of Mahmoud dismissing to them daughters as what she asked, but they caused that to recklessness and stupidity in Mr.

Mahmoud behavior been time by time!, Maria felt regret for her relative.

Mahmoud took his car and went to Barnous home to carry back his relative, the Barnouss felt honor when Mahmoud came to them home, for that they hoped him to enter, all the family came to the door front to asking him to enter, to drink something at least, he had fallen in shame for them insistence requests and asking, they rounded him in circle, everybody from his side asking him with pleasure to enter them home, he has not any chance to leave them back without his stranger relative, then he entered to them salon among welcoming from all, even them friend the taxi driver, Maria was sat on rich place as a queen, near table of drinks and sweets, the taxi driver sat beside her to translate and explain everything to her.

Mahmoud doesn't wants facing his hosts, for that he apologized to them, he caused the dismissing reason to his work exhaustion which made him became angry and nerves, Barnouss knew that he was lied, but they accepted his apologized with pleasure, then everybody in the salon applauded him, Mahmoud was wondered at all them clamor and noise, Barnouss have an unknown behavior with strangers, who they meeting them for first time, he surprised with more shame feeling when the two young-girls jumped on his knees shameful dresses kissing and hugging him among high applause as a declaration of the problem end, Barnouss know that Mr. Mahmoud was a respected man from every quarter rudder, so when they could get his sympathize with them then them reputation in quarter will be in high.

Barnouss have a skill to get sympathize and love of everybody entering them home, they trained themselves to satisfy any wishes or needs of everybody entering them home, as a servers or slaves, them job is comforting, and entertainment everybody, they do not be nervous for any reason, doing everything with smile and fun, the behavior of the entertainment professionals people, for that they were the best place for everybody needs fun and entertainment without any limitation.

Sozan sent Salma and Azza to follow Mr. Mahmoud when he was late, they entered the family salon with The mother welcoming been, the Barnous sisters intended to show them sitting on Mr. Mahmoud knees and kissing him to Salma and Azza, after when they knew that Azza and Salma saw them in that position stood-up with fun and hugged them hardly with noise talk and joking.

Maria been relax while she saw all that family sympathy anywhere around, Mrs. Mahmoud still in his shame fell been, his forehead has been flowing a cold sweat, Salma and Azza looking each other with smiles as they are see a film without title, every thing was changed in minutes, Mrs. Mahmoud in whores hugs and kissing, all of them became in Barnous forbidden home on face of everybody, the no respected family have been them host, but the two clever girls took that as a chance to get some fun.

Madam Barnous gave her guests some fruit-juice cups and some sweets, Mahmoud drunk his cup quickly and stood-up to take leave of, the family asked him to spend more time but he apologized to them, Maria did not wants go with them, then the family promised Mahmoud to associated with her to his home whenever she wants, then Mahmoud with his daughter and her friend left the home back by Mahmoud is car.

In Mahmoud home the two friends told Sozan all what was happened with joking, but Mahmoud went directly to his bedroom without anymore word.

Sozan found every her around actions was been strange, she did not knew why her sister Maria left them home and associated with the two bad girls to them home?, and stayed there refused coming-back home!, the sitting of the Barnous sisters in her husband hold with them kisses and hugs!, why Mahmoud did that!, why he did not carried back her sister without entering them home at all?, why he became nerve when he found them in his home and after that he became them guest?, she knew well her husband, he was serious and honest, never did any shame doing, so what was happened?, everything became strange.

Fatma came to Bera home to carried back her daughter Azza, Sozan talked with her about what was happened frankly, they were friends before long time, loved each other, she told here about her sister Maria unintentional doing when she welcomed the wrong people, her doing put her family from bad to bad acts, Fatma imagined everything was happened, encouraged Sozan to be strong and to explain the happening to her neighbors, because in sure that they saw her family entered to Barnouss home!.

Maria have been knowing some of her around happening slowly, she was enjoyed with Barnouss family who they asked her to eat dinner in them home, Mr. Mohammed informed her about them nearly church, she was happy when she knew that there is a church nearly, Maria loved Mohammed after hate, he was funny and easy man, the mother told her by smile through the translator Mohammed that she is free to do or ask everything, when Mahmoud translated that for her she winked her and kissed her lips with high laughing and carried her to her bedroom, Maria surrendered for her, she asked and encouraged her to take-off her wears. Maria in commencement refused her ask, but after Najat insistence been she decided to surrendered for her again, at least to know what she does wants to do for her, Najat laid Maria on the bed who dressed just her underwear, on her front side and anointed her back by massage cream which brought, and massaged her body back, neck and shoulders, Maria never felt like that feeling, Najat trained hands wandered on every her deep back binders, she felt a great pleasure streamed in all her body, then when Najat laid her back on her body back she was swimming in pleasure pool, her eyes were closed, her mouth opened out-of controlling, as an big soft doll, Najat took-of her underwear too, and completed massage all her upside front body, that made Maria deeply in un-sensation status, after that she covered her by a nice perfumed blanked and let her in pleasure dreams.

After that Najat with the two daughters going to cook dinner, many ladies and men came while Maria pleasure dream, Sozan decided go with herself to carry back her sister, it does not good that she spent all that time in an unknown people home, All the Family came to them home front to welcoming to them Italian neighbor, they did as what they were did to her husband Mahmoud, she tried to let them called her sister but the asking of them made her in shame too, she entered with full welcoming wards and acts can be do, as a queen came to look her people, that overdoing of welcoming made her in more shame, all of the salon sitters welcomed her with applause and hello, there is many people in the salon drinking and joking noisily, Sozan did not saw her sister in the salon, then she asked Najat with shame low voice about her sister, Najat informed her that her sister in rest for some time, and asked here to make herself home, without shame, that large welcoming amazed Sozan and made her in good feeling also the two girls kissed and hugged her many times, really that family has an unknown power to change everybody to be in an magical nice mode, they were specialist in entertainment field, nobody could be away of them effects.

Sozan spent some fun time with the family, drinks some valuable fruit-juice cups, she forgot the cause of her coming, every thing in Barnous home was peaceful, everybody were happy and clear, the general condition encourages everybody to forget himself, Najat and the sisters asked Sozan to be with them in the kitchen where they cooking food to them guests, them kitchen was large and comfort contains every food kinds, she was happy that the Barnouss considered her as a special one can be in them kitchen, then she was happy in time of sharing them efforts of cooking, in same time of exchanging some dirty jokes with Najat and her daughters, who passed her many funny jests never she heard before, made her in deep laughing hurts her body sides and watered her eyes, never done since long time, after more time Sozan remembered her coming reason, then she asked Najat to carry her to her sister place, but Najat asked her with laugh to make herself home. one time more, and pushed her with joking indicated to one of faced rooms.

In Najat bedroom Sozan found her sister been in deep sleep covered by comfortable nice blanket, she sat beside her and waking up her by low voice, after few minutes she woke up silently and smiled when she saw her sister beside her, Sozan smiled too with thanks Allah that she was well, Maria sat in her place and stretched her hands in high forgot that she was naked, Sozan turned her head far of her naked sister then she saw her sister clothes on chair beside the bed, all her clothes, even her underwear, Maria she felt happy and light, then she covered her breasts with laugh and explaining talk to her sister:

- Madam Najat massaged my body, she is a professional masseur, I never found someone like her or felt like this feeling before, she is wonderful, she re-made me .. oh Sozan how made me an other person.

Sozan became too happy for her sister good mood, but in her self secret she condemned her sister naked in a strangers home, she hugged her and stood up talking with laugh:

- You spending happy time here while I was worried about you!.

Maria said with surely voice:
- Nothing bad here!, I am happy that I met people like them, I loved them deeply my sister.

Sozan asked her sister to wear her clothes and left the room to the kitchen, where Najat and her daughters received her by them joking noise and dance, after few minutes Maria came to kitchen too, seem happy and comforted, she hugged Najat with many thanks for her massage done, Najat kissed again her lips and welcoming here with some tickle, the two daughters hugged her too and kissed her on her lips too, Sozan asked Najat permission to leave with her sister, although them warm requests to delay them leave after dinner, Sozan insists to leave, then the ladies escorted them to them home door, on the salon step Sozan and Maria said good-bye to everybody, on the door step Najat and her daughters hugged Sozan and Maria, they left Barnouss after sure promised them to come-back to them in the future and don't forget them.

On night, when Faris came back home from Masjed found three unknown people waiting him in his house corner, they called him by his name, he came to them closely but he did not knew anyone, he had shaking hands with them, one of them smiled to Faris and said with a calm voice:
- Dear Faris, you don't know us, but we know you well, you are a religious Youngman and we are respecting and trust you as a faithful man, are we in right?.

Faris surprised, he thought that these people need asking for some one or whatever, but they seemed as they are came to him directly for unknown something, but he smiled with embarrassment and welcomed them to continue, the man completed:

- Ok .. frankly, we are a people from (Islamic front) and we need your help to do something for Allah.. just some help .. very easy and safe if you want!.

The man stopped talking when he did not felt any zeal, Faris was calm listening every word carefully, but when the man stopped he gathered himself and said:

- Thank you for your trust, but I am not a political man, I am just someone unemployed waiting my chance!, I have not any experience to help myself until I can help others, I am sorry!.

Other one from the three who was listened said with laugh:

- You are frankly man too Faris, your chance is with us, we can help you more than you think, you are a good man and we asked you to try to help us for Allah, you will not repent of anything, you are surprised, we will comeback to you tomorrow, but we don't want warn you to let this meetings in secret even your mother and sister, please don't forget.

Faris: Ok.. don't worry, there is nothing to say!.

The three young-men shook hands with Faris and left him to the dark while Faris entered his home with confused mind.

Faris did not informed his mother or sister about what happened in them home front before few minutes, sat in home hall eating his dinner looking to his mother and sister who watched TV with quiet, his mind busy try to understand what is the point of the strange visiting!, and what was that easy safe help they asked him to do?, and why him from of the quarter young-men?.

Sozan with Maria and Salma in them home salon drunk tea and talking about Barnouss nice welcoming and behavior, while Mahmoud in his room lonely watch TV and thinking about the big Maria fault which led them to be friends with bad family.

Barnouss are too happy, that they did a new relationship with Mahmoud family that will open the closed doors to be an admitted family in them around.

Someone sat on dark over a tree on front spy on the church.

Other one came to Masjed Imam to inform him about Mahmoud family visiting to Barnouss.

Nearly, in dark home there was three men around a table drunk tea and talked with whisper.

Police car wandered about homes watching quarter traffic.

———

(4)
Mr. Bobo

Day after, about ten o clock in the morning, the quarter road was calm, warm sun arose over white clouds, some children playing on road grass, everything was perfect in that day, last night Maria was agreed with Mohammed Lamin to carry her to church, Mohamed came in time in front of her home and piped, Sozan hurried to Maria when she saw her get ready to leave home, Maria informed her that she is going to visit the church with Mohammed the taxi driver who talked with him last night, Sozan felt bad that her young sister did not informed her last night about her visit, Maria smile for her and Salma and take leave of them hurrying to the taxi.

Farida was babies doctor, a friend of Salma, lives nearly, exchanges visiting with Salma time to time, came that morning to visit her friend Salma, she saw her aunt hurrying to taxi and went away, Sozan lose herself control, anger made her as a crazy she shut down the door with force and yelled curses to her absent sister Maria described her by dirty descriptions, Salma was laughed when she saw her mother full angry, she did not saw her mother been crazy before like that day, she seemed as someone will burst, her mother described her sister as a whore, selfish, stupid, aimless, haughty, but shortly she stopped when she heard the door bell rings, she climbed the stairs to her bedroom while Salma went to door.

Salma smiled when she found her lovely friend on her steps, she hugged her and welcomed her to enter, Farida asked her about her mother crying, Salma told her with laughing about her aunt going to church without any advance inform which made her mother crazy.

While Mohammed waiting in outside, Maria entered the church from corner door, which led her directly to the main hall, Maria knelt in front of Christ statue and prayed.

In church Maria acquainted with Mr. Bobo the church supervisor, who welcomed Maria by his little English language and invited her to come at the next Sunday to pray with them, he was an Arabian Christian, he wandered with her in the church, Maria surprised when Mr. Bobo informed her that he knows Mr. Mahmoud and his family, because Mr. Mahmoud invited all church Christians many times to his home for many occasions!, Maria did not knew the reason of her unhappy feeling when Mr. Bobo informed her about Mahmoud and his family as known good people!, in herself felt bad, she thought that the church is special for her because she was Christian, why Muslims like her relative Mahmoud?, and why Mr. Bobo and his Christians company accepted Mahmoud invitations?, that turbulence feeling pushed her went-out the church to the taxi as a drunk one angry, without Mr. Bobo farewell, sat in the taxi and asked Mr. Mohammed to wander her around.

Mohammed carried her around the quarter where she saw through the windows many nice places, suddenly she saw the Barnous sisters walking with two boys, she asked Mohammed to stop for them, the two girls left them friends and jumped into the car laughing noisy as usually, Mohammed carried them for short trip and returned to Maria home, Maria invited the two girls to spend some time with her, so they raced to the door who be the first one rings the bell, Salma face became yellow when she saw her aunt with the two Barnous sisters, but she has nothing to do, just she controlled herself and welcomed them to enter!.

Dr. Farida surprised when she saw Barnous sisters with Maria entered the salon with laughing noisy, the two girls jumped to embracing Salma and Farida and with more impudence they tried kissing them lips, among defense of the two friends to push them faces softly far of them, Salma presented her friend to her aunt and inverse, after that Maria invited her two new friends to her bedroom and left them with noisy.

Farida after sat down for moments said with low voice as some one breathing with difficulty:
- What was that Salma?, How you let your aunt knows or going with Barnouss?, are you crazy?, they are as dogs excrete in any place!,

Salma were in same anger, sat down looked to her friend with yellow smile, and replied her asking:
- My aunt has not any bad information about Barnouss, and she is stubborn person doing as she like without any advance informing, then she led us to some troubles , All my family are angry because of her,

you saw my mother status, she is disturbing aunt, we don't want hurt her, but I think our patience been was emptied!, we must stop her!.. and we will!.

Farida spent some more time with her friend and left out returned to her home.

Maria enjoying with the two sisters in her room, they laughed her deeply, Maria did not stopped them when they tickled her breasts, but she laid her body back on the bed with laugh noisy as what they done to make a space for them tickles, she was in top enjoyment when Salma knocked the door carried a tray gathered some drinks and cakes, she surprised when she heard her aunt asked her to leave away back with nervy voice, Salma get back to kitchen, now she know that her aunt became closed with the two sisters, and if she don't returning her mind never she will be back, she felt that those girls will break them life.

Faris when he returned to his home at noon get a closed envelope carried by someone gave to his mother waiting for him, he surprised when he opened it, mother also was worry to see what that strange envelope contains, she surprised too when Faris put all contents over the table, it was some money and letter, the letter was an official government letter informed him that he is accepted as an employee with a government company, asked him to attaché his job as possible as soon, while he surprised he accounted the money it is a big amount, Fatma snatched the letter, and read it, she was completely in happiness, she jumped to her son kissing him with cry and thanks Allah who gave her son a chance to build his future, Faris hugged her mother too and cries, in that time

Azza came back home too, all the family became glad, the gladness forgot them the source of the money!, and who was brought it to them home with the job letter?.

Fatma asked her son about the unknown man who brought the envelope, Faris was worry too, he remembered his last night visitors, did them who been behind the work acceptance letter and the money?. He remember the talking of the last talker which meant that they can help him more than he think!, yes those people helped them more than he think!, never the letter came with itself!, he was waiting this letter two years with no chance been , but someone brought it in one day!, what is the power of those people had!, and if they had all this power and money why they need his little help?, all that questions turned in his mind as hammers when his mother asked him about the source of the money and who was that unknown person who brought it?.

Faris can not informs his mother the reality, he promised them, so he informed her that he guessed that someone friend made a surprise for him, he will know him soon, then the mother smiled and uttered with high voice with made Azza laughing with high and try to utter too, while Faris looking them with smile.

Souzan got some sleep and descended down to prepare lunch, Salma succeeded her to the kitchen, she was more nervy when Salma informed her that the Barnous sisters with her sister in her bedroom, Mourad and Ali who attached them mother and sister in the kitchen, they were nervy too, the two ladies worked for lunch while the two guys sat beside the kitchen table, all of them had been thinking in the same subject, them aunt doings, they were seemed, hopeless, worried, as someone been in trap do not able to jumps away, finally Salma while she is moving said with Italian language:

- Someone must stop her, her doings brought the misery to this house, all of us became sad, everyday she made a new stupid doing ..

All of them became as statues when Maria entered the kitchen suddenly and told Salma with nervy voice:

- Who brought misery to this family?.

Salma surprised but she encouraged her self looking to her aunt and said:

- You brought misery to this family!.

Maria did not believed her ears, she listened all what Salma said before her entered, she guessed that she was talking about her, but never she can guess that Salma will face her, Maria shocked, her anger showed on her face, her body trembled, her angry wave be bigger than her chest space, looked to Salma and screamed with high voice as a thunder:

- Me!, .. whore .. are you a family?, you are nothing!, you are enemies of Christ!, you are stupid Muslims, dirty idolaters, I hate all of you!.

Salma with the two guys left the kitchen to them rooms silently, while Sozan sat on one of the kitchen chair cries silently too, Maria left back too to her room and shut down her room door with force made the home windows shivered.

The door bell rung suddenly, Sozan washed her face quickly and went to the door, Mr. Bobo were there, Sozan surprised, she did not saw him before long time, but she welcomed him with fade smile.

In salon Mr. Bobo informed her about her sister visit to the church, he was worried because she left the church without Farewell as someone runaway with worry, he came to reassure about her!.

Souzan reassured him about her sister that maybe she was in hurry or remembered something to do but she is fine, nothing lead to worry, and thanked him too much for his coming and invited him to stay to take lunch with them, but the man said goodbye to her and left the house.

The two sisters was in Maria bedroom listened every word said, and saw Maria came back to them, she left them to bring some drinks, but she came back sad and nervy, so they asked her to leave home, when Maria became lonely laid her body on bed, she was nerves but she became happy too, she found her happiness was strange, she felt that she been light when she said all that talking to her sister family, that sentences were in her breast need to go out, she smiled for herself and jumped out the bed to make shower.

On lunch table Maria was absent, she informed her sister that she wasn't hungry, the family ate them lunch silently, looking each other with sad eyes.

After lunch one of Barnous sisters came back to Maria to inform her that the Barnouss invited her to be them guest for any time long she need if she is not happy in her sister home, Maria knew that the sisters informed them parent that Maria does not happy in her sister house, so they invited her to them home, that *action made Maria happy, that she has a friends felt her sense and going to help her!.*

Sozan decided speak out frankly to Maria, so she went to her room and knocked the door many times but Maria did not replied, Sozan worried, knocked the door more hard but no answer, her worry been more and more, she thought that there is some thing bad happened to her sister, she called her with high voice by her name to open the door, Sozan try to open the locked door with force but she failed, the door was strong, she sought help of them sons, the two sons came followed with Salma, all of them yelled to Maria to open the locked door but there is no answer, Mourad brought a hammer and broke the lock by strong blows, all of them was surprised when the door opened, Maria had been sitting down calm on the bed, she had been looking to them with large smile, Sozan sat on the floor crying with high voice slapping her face and head, the sons were stopped as statues looked for them aunt by dead eyes.

Sons left the place with no single word, Sozan cleaned her eyes by her robe sleeve and looked to her sister through her eyes teardrops from her down sitting and said with calm voice:

- Maria why you do this stupid acts?,.. what do you want?.. I am your sister and they are your lonely family .. we are orphans .. no other body cares about us! .. please open your chest to me and inform me what happen? .. why you are angry?, .. please tell me!.

Maria did not said any thing, she still sat looking her sister with large smile, as she did not heard or saw any thing!.

After few minutes with no single word exchanged, Sozan stood up and progressed to Maria gathered her force and slapped her face by strong blow fell her down the bed, her nose bled, Maria screamed by high voice damning her sister while handles her nose and looking to her sister by fired eyes, and stood up to fight with her, Sozan slapped her again overthrew her in the room corner, Maria cried with high voice and screamed described Sozan by every bad dirty words, touching her face and nose, showing her blood on her hands, while Sozan stood us looking her with stony eyes, Maria feared, she did not guessed that her sister is very strong, she can kill her in minutes, for that she stopped screaming, she contented with calm cry with full scare, Sozan looked to her and said with calm voice:

Please listen to me carefully .. every word I will speak is true hundred percent, I supposed that you were been lonely for long time .. loneliness made you a savage person!, sickened your mind and senses, I didn't imagined that your status became to this dangerous level!, you are as a really crazy person!, none cared you in the past, but I am your old sister as your mother .. I will do the best for you!, you have wrong ideas about us, none enemy here!, not for Christ!, not for Christians!, not for everybody!, all those people in the home or outside home none of them is the Christ enemy, they believed in Christ more than you did .. yes .. of course .. there is some one here or there is crazy like you, every religions has some extremists believe in ungodly ideals, invite to hate and damage like you! ... but they are criminals .. all of them are criminals! .. do you want be one of them?.. Islam is a good religion .. Islam ordered Muslims to wish every good thing to everybody as what they wish that for themselves! .. Muslims do not dirty, they clean them selves five times per day, and have been praying five times per day, you are yourself enemy, Barnouss are a suspicious family, they have been drinking liquor, using drugs and hallucination tablets, Najat and her daughters are whores, make entertainments for public without any limitation, everybody can fuck them in anytime, for that Mahmoud tried to drive away them but because of you, that we didn't wanted to hurt your feeling .. we entered them home and dealt with them as a good neighbors, all our neighbors blamed us, we are a respected family do not like that .. all of our good neighbors and friends dealt with you as them sister, gave presents to you, because they guessed that you are a good person .. part of respected family .. they did not cared about your religion or where you are from !.. they looked to you as a human brother of them, who what you are! .. the religion is your personal connection with your God, no respected religion invited people to hate or damage the others .. God or Allah never invited them believers to damage or hurt everybody who is in same religion or no!.. if you understood this words deeply you will be aright, if you didn't, you will be in criminal way .. the prison will be your ever home .. please .. please understand me, never I will let you be in the in jail or Mind-sanatorium!.

She said that while Maria still listening without any reaction, looking her sister with scare showed on her face and eyes, after that Sozan asked Maria to stand, when she did, Sozan led her to bathroom where cleaned her face and changed her bloody robe by cleaned dress and drove her to the kitchen, when Maria tried to say something she ordered her to quiet, Maria stopped try talk, and followed her as a baby follows his mother, she sat her behind the kitchen table and put apposite here some food and drink and ordered her to eat, Maria ate and drank with greedy, after that she led her to salon and opened TV for her to an entertainment Italian channel and left her there with no more word.

Sozan phoned Sami who was a friend of her sons, the quarter homes maintenance technician to fix the broken door, after few minutes he came with his tools box and fixed it in little more minutes became as new one while Maria in her place watching TV and every movement with full attention while her little mind repeating her sister full last long talk.

Maria found strange in her sister talking, she talked as her friend Maurice who is in Milan, Sozan did not knew Maurice but they have the same viewpoint, Maria mind did not accepted that the right has no nationality, the right is same, Is she crazy?, is she extremist?, are Sozan and Maurice in the right and she and Mss. Bella and Mr. George in Milan were in wrong?, Christ ordered his believers to love them enemies as the lord of Muslims as what Sozan said!, she has not information about Islam she was ought to learn Islam before her coming, but she has not a time and able to understand Islam or Christ religion well!, she wants head lines without details, details needs stable sense which she has not!, she is as a soldier without mind, just indicate the enemy to him so he will fight him without questions, she don't want tires her mind!, some times she feel that the world is too complex for some people like her, she wants believe her sister but her sister is a Muslim so she guess that she is not honest, but Maurice wasn't Muslim!, who knows?, perhaps he was Muslim in secret!, when she was in Milan everything was clear, but here every ideas became complex!.

Maria felt that she lost her sister and her family respect and love, also when she descend to her room, the door was fixed but no key in the inside lock, her sister took the key, now she felt that she lost her privacy too, that is too easy for her to apologize to her sister family, but she did not, and she did not think about that, her sister slaps feared her, she remembered her mother slaps which she was young and made something wrong, she was strong and calm like Souzan, she ought to deem all what Sozan talked was lie, but Sozan said that all what she said was true hundred per cent!, Is it true that Islam a good religion like Christianity and has many more details?, and there is no enemy for Christ here or any Muslims lands?, is she an Christian extremist as some Muslims extremists?, is she a criminal as them?, is the jail will be her ever home?, she was sad and tired, then she closed her door and lay on the bed try to sleep.

Mahmoud assembled a new control cameras to let everyone in home can see outside the home easy and clear, his neighbors looked to him by sorrow eyes, they don't want them new relation with Barnouss but none talked him about that, but he knew them sorrow cause, he talked with his wife about Maria new stupid doing, Souzan reassured him without details that Maria will be tranquil, she ordered her sons to do not informed them father about what them aunt done or said to do not load Mahmoud more worry.

The home phone rang, Mss. Bella was online talking from Milan wants to talk with Maria, Souzan ascend to inform Maria who woke up and hurried to get her room phone, Souzan found strange her sister suddenly vivacity and happiness, she was completely other one, Maria looked to her to let her alone but Souzan pretended to be as did not understood and stilled stood behind her to listen, Maria did not liked that but she continued talking while she try to make the microphone far of Souzan, but Souzan listened ever single word, Mss. Bella informed her that someone will come to her tomorrow with some Arabic Gospel copies, and asked her about what she done in her past days, Maria promised her that everything will be alright.

Souzan asked her about her communed?, and who will come tomorrow with the Gospel copies?, Maria smiled and told her with unusually calm voice mixed with sarcasm:
- Look my sister, every Saracen must be become Christian in this land, I am one of team who serving the lord Christ to Christianize every Libyan!.
Souzan laughed with high voice:
- Really You are crazy Maria!.
She said that and left the room laughing clapped her hands.

Maria said in secret:
- *We will see who will laugh in the end!.*   *The Imam came to Mahmoud shortly to preach to him about them new relationship with Barnouss, Mahmoud reassured him that there is no new relationship with Barnouss, all the story that his strange relative has not any advance bad information about them, the Barnouss took the opportunity to visit her and carried her to them home, Masjed Imam became happy and left Mahmoud, Mahmoud seems to him as a lead man, never done shame.*

Day next, at ten o clock, Mr. Bobo came to Mahmoud home, he showed by the cameras from the inside, Souzan found strange his coming, but she opened the door, after exchanging salutes, Mr. Bobo informed Sozan that he came to see Mss Maria lonely, Sozan called Maria to come down, Maria and Mr. Bobo sat with Sozan in the salon, Mr. Bobo looked to Sozan to left them alone but Sozan stilled in her sit and said to him:
- *Mr. Bobo there is no secret in this home, Maria is my sister and she came to Libya on the basis of my official invitation, she is under my responsibility, for that there is no secret here!.*

Mr. Bobo surprised, he said by stutter voice:
- *But this is her business!.*

Sozan with firmness:
- *I invited her to spend some time under family invitation law, not to do any business, also I knew about the Gospel copies!, are you the man who must carry them to her?.*

Mr. Bobo said with more stutter:

- Oh .. yes there is someone carried them in big envelop to the church and asked me to deliver them to her, the envelope is in the church.

Maria felt that she and Mr. Bobo in same front, a Christian front against enemy front!, for that she said with angry to her sister:

- I am not you slave, I am Christian and this is my church observer a....

Souzan cut her talk with strong voice:

- Shut you mouth .. stupid! ... if you want to be free of my responsibility go back to Italy and you can come back without my family invitation law status, then you will be free to do as you like, but now you will do as what I will order to you, no more no less!.

Mr. Bobo nodded his head as an agreeing to Sozan talking, Maria felt down, she asked Mr. Bobo with un-believed voice:

- What? .. did she said the truth?.

- Yes .. she did!, You are under her personal responsibility!, you came her under family meeting law, not to do any social business, if you are going to do some other things then go back to Italy and return with other kind of visa!.

Maria looked to them with unrelieved eyes, does she can not move for every thing just with her sister order?.. as a baby! .. without free-will! .. Mr. Bobo asked Sozan to come tomorrow to the church to receive the envelop of her sister if she want, he said that and hoped a nice day for them and left them out, while Maria jumped mounted the stairs to her room.

Souzan saw that she must inform her husband about all Maria stories to help her to found a safe way to do the best!.

Mahmoud listened carefully to his wife, but he stilled in his sit without any reaction, Sozan asked him to say something, then he looked to her with sad eyes and hugged her strongly and said:

- As what you said she is a part of team exploited her family visiting to Christianize the people here!, maybe more things!, Mr. Bobo is a balanced man, really Christian man, your sister will damage him by her irresponsible doing, but ok .. we can help her to do what she want to do by family meetings, that will be make her safe, if she wants! .. go and ask her, if she accepted our support we will make a special family program for her to talk with people about her religion in safe!.

Sozan knew her husband, but always she look a nice new sides in his perfect character!, she went to her sister who was in her bed watching TV, Sozan smile for her and said:

- Ok Mss. Maria you can meet people and talk to them about your religion to be Christians or whatever you want!.

Maria surprised, she reduced the TV voice and turned her face to her sister with opened eyes screaming:

- What did you said?

Sozan repeated her talking:

- Yes Mahmoud will help you to invite people to be Christians!.

- Mahmoud will help me to serve my lord!.

- Yes, Just now he sent me to you to accept his support to help you if you want!.
- How?.
- He can make for you a family meetings to talk with people about your religion!.
       Maria said with confused voice:
- A family meetings!
Sozan simply:
- Yes, You can said everything and the people will hear and discuss you!.
       Maria with frustration:
- Is this a new trick from you and your husband?
       Sozan said with patient:
- No .. there is no trick .. really we can help you in the law space!.
- You are Muslims, and want help me to Christianize your people?
       Sozan with more patient:
- Yes!, because Mahmoud and I believed that every body is free to choose her personality needs, wrong or right, his chosen is his business, if he asking our advise we can advise him, if he does not, we do not care .. he is free to do with himself as he likes or wishes if his doings has not any general reactions or touching others.
       Maria took her body back think with turned away eyes, while Sozan waiting her reply.

-----

(5)
Brotherhood

Not so far from church there is a simple house hidden by vegetables, has negligent front , but its inside was comfortable, in one of its rooms around a big table Faris sat with his last unknown three visitors, they called him for meeting before short time, they indicated him to the hidden house, this is the first time he noted this building, it seem as a deserted house, but he liked its interior, they presented themselves to Faris as Ayyad, Maher, Salem, they where young-men older than Faris, Faris guessed what they will talk with him about, he was waited them connection with patience after he received them money and the job letter two days ago.

He remembered them faces and talk, Salem was the last one who told him that (they can help him more than he think!), he is talking with trusted accent as a leader, Maher was the first one talked older than all of them, nice and calm, Ayyad is as a silent man, has not much talk.

Maher was the first one talked to Faris with nice smile:
- Ok .. brother Faris I think you have to say something!.

Faris looking to them together and said with calm voice:
- At first .. thank you for your care, I received your money and your job letter which is in my pocket now, I

am a man believed in Allah that who can make me rich or poor, no one can buy me, I am not for sale, I know that you want help me, but with condition, I don't need help with conditions, that is not for Allah, Allah order us to help others without conditions, You proved to me your power, I waited this letter two years, you brought it in some hours, and you came to my home needed my poor help!, are you kid with me? , You do not need my help, you have money and power, what do you wish for?.

Faris said this talk and took out from his pocket the envelope which contains the money and the letter and put it on the table.

The three young-men stood up suddenly greeted Allah by high voice with waved them fists three times and rushed to Faris kissing and hugging him, Faris completely surprised, he did not apprehended them act!, he been hurry to be ready to fight them, he guessed that they are going to do something wrong for him, after they did what they done they returned back to them sits with calm crying, while Faris was in frozen stand looking around him with astonishment.

The three young-men cleaned them eyes carefully, Salem saw to Faris and said with his calm deep voice:

- Brother Faris .. really we are happy that there is someone like you, what you done today is repeating to what I done long time ago at the first contact with the Islam front party, and these my two brothers was there too, The Islam always renew his blood by new honest sure people like you, never accepts the wrong, he can die been hungry but never longing her hand to bad

earn, brother Faris we did not helped you to bend you, or to exploit your situation, we helped you for Allah only, because you are a good Muslim, never done any shame, for that we helped you, we invited you today to inform you about our party and answer all your questions, we want you to be one of us, or you can refuse everything and you can be as a friend and brother to us, no more no less.. is my talk clear our brother Faris?

Salem talk took out every misunderstands in Faris mind, them doing became clear, they did not invited him to bargain with him, if them help to Allah without any conditions he will accept it, he put back the envelope to his pocket and sat down on his chair and said:

- Brother Salem as what I told you before .. I am not a political person.. I am a Youngman in my life beginning, have nothing, I have not any thing more than others, I must spend a long time in work to build my life, the Islam is my religion not my craft, I don't want pass my family money in my needs, politics needs men who had power and money like you, how I can benefit your party if I have nothing, I want short the way for you to understand my situation, I received your help because you said that you did that for Allah, without conditions, if not, there is no problem, I have Allah will help me!.

When Faris finished his talk, the silence been covered the place, Maher smiled to Faris and said:

- please Attention Faris, if everybody said like you now, that he must build his life before care to Muslims situations so nobody will care, because everybody

always have new thing to do seem for him as an important needs, human is needy, always need more things showed for him as an important things, Muslims is a satisfied person, Muslims young-men fight everywhere, anywhere, with silence, every body of them has a personal life and needs, but they left all those needs and wishes in them back and went ahead to withstood the injustice of the Muslims enemies, you are one of this great nation, your grand fathers came here to north Africa had nothing, just them religion to lead idolaters who they had been worshipped statues, to the light, to worship Allah, they did not said like you, now, and thought about themselves needs, and did not cared about them humans brothers, so you ought to be one of the idolaters, married you mother or fuck you sister or daughter or drink to steal or kill your neighbors .. is this the life you have been wishing?

Faris bent his head over his hands which opened on the table, Maher talk was very logically, yes if everybody do like him so nobody will care the general situation of the Muslims, Faris he uplifted his head and said:
- Firstly, who gave you the right to care the Muslims general situation?, this is the Muslims governments duties!, and who are the Muslims enemies?, and how you will fight them?... an..
Salem said with laugh cut Faris talk:
- Wait .. wait .. these three questions together !, I will replay you after tea drink.
All of them laughed in high, Salem went to the kitchen brought a tray contain thermos of tea and milk and plate of sweets, they drank tea with laughs and

some kidding, Salem stopped kidding and said directed his face to Faris:

- What is you first question?

Faris replied Salem seriously:

- Who gave you the right to care the Muslims general situation?

Salem laughed and said seriously too:

- Firstly .. you are a brave man .. Ok .. Brother .. Muslims land now is separated, Muslims are not one hand, became nations not one nation as what Islam ordered, led by bad governors, loved the present-life, they don't care but themselves, the west and the east had no mercy for us, they exploited our weaken after strength to sow bad families who was agreed with them to be our governors!, .. so there is not really governors can make a really forward the Muslims status to be in the front, as you can see two milliards Muslims could not stopped the philistine colonialism, and many aggressions against Muslims and them lands .. a..

Faris cut Salem saying:

- Dear .. you are accounting the reasons .. but my question was: Who did gave you the power to be the Muslims deputy? .. no one gave you competences or made you to be the Muslims agent?.

Salem with calm voice:

*- You did not let me complete my speech .. ok ..The Islam .. the Koran and The Sunna (*The Mohammed mode: his speeches and doings), who gave the Muslims the right to correct any wrong!, a..*

Faris cut his talk said:

- But who can judges the doings is it wrong or right? .. who have the right to say this is wrong or right .. to

make a final judgment for everything .. Koran and Sunna led Muslims to respect Muslims governors!, an..

Salem cut Faris talking:

- You are searching for excuses to disavow from your responsibilities to Islam and Muslims!

Faris with pressed voice:

- No, that is not true! .. we are here to discuss your ideas, I knew Koran and Sunna well, so I need your large patient to reach the truth, if no you are free to complete!.

Salem had no gotten angry, he stilled calm, he stood and took a chair far of Faris, Maher smile to Faris and said:

- Look Faris .. you are thinking quickly .. we know that you are scared .. and you have many enquires .. but let us tell you our viewpoints and then you can ask .. ok!.

Faris said with some nerve:

- Do you brought me here to listen to you? .. this is not right .. do you want me hear you and left you alone? .. I can do that .. but this is not right too!.

Salem said:

- No .. no .. you have to give us a chance to tell you the truth! .. do not cut our speech.

Faris:

- I know the truth!, who told you others but you do not know the truth? .. I have a mind like you can lead me to the right!, accept me as what I am not as you like!, this is the right culture, you accept only as you like, me, I accept who is as he likes, I am not he or you or every body, and you are in the same status, the difference between me and you that you made yourself a judge to impose your viewpoint to others, if he is

looking to the world as you looking you will class him in (like) (position) if he has other viewpoints, so he will be in (unlike) (position), or as an enemy in other explaining!.

Salem:
- I don't know, how you are been Muslim and you have been saying this speech?.
Faris:
- Why?, I am a Muslim but I look to the world as one union, humans became bigger than of any selfish or narrow viewpoints, all worldwide peoples talking together frankly and in deep!, everybody has the right to be as he like or wish, no one licensed to close them mouths or eyes, the people culture became high, except some people do not want to understand!.

Maher said laughing:
- Some people like us!.

Faris with shame:
- No .. no .. please .. I did not mean that!, I mean everybody did not noted the growing and renewing of the nations culture, which begat understanding never had been at previous time.
Salem:
- Do you think that the Islam became an old think?.

Faris:
- No .. Islam made the base of the human think, but he gave the right to the next generations to behave, per example, Omar Ebn-Alkhattab was the second governor of Muslims who made the first government in Islam history, he parted the responsibilities, as a ministries now, (Divans), one for military, one for commerce -markets administration- , one of treasury ..

est., that government system did not denied from Mohammed company who were in life in that time!, Al - jihad originally was (the holy fight to publish the Islam culture), in full right words was to fight every partition stands between people and Islam knowledge, for that you see many not Muslims in Muslims land, because no one obliged them to be Muslims!, the first Muslims just broke the limitations (who was the governments) between them and Islam culture, if they wanted to be Muslims or no that is not a problem, many of them became Muslims, some of them still in them old religions, after second world war the situation had changed, now there is no partitions, you can publish the Islam culture without fight, with Radios, TV, Press, books, no blocked ways, all ways opened on your face, did not been before, for that (Al Jihad) stopped, because the reason of (Al Jihad) was gone, if someone talk about (Al Jihad) for other reason, then that is no (Jihad), he will talk about other kinds of fights not Jihad that is the Muslims holy fight for Allah, to make his speech in heard, Just for Allah, old Muslims had understood the limits of Allah orders.

Maher:

- that is true, but as you see also Christians elaborated them religion publishing, we are near of an Christians Church in Muslims land.

Faris:

- Why not?, everybody have the right to practice his religion pray in church, in Masjed everywhere, in anywhere!.

Salem:

- In briefly, you see that (Al Jihad) was blocked!, and everybody must be accepted as what who was been!, and the Muslims responsible are them governors good or bad!, am I alright?

Faris:

- Yes.

Salem:

- Ok, You are a man has a large culture, so you need long time discussing, then we will finish our meeting with you today, and we will continue in future meeting.

Faris with calm voice:

- Do I have to come?

Salem said with amazement:

- Don't you want come?.

Faris:

- I am indebted to you for your help, but I don't want come back for any future discussion meeting, I have to go to my new work and see to do my business!.

Salem said with laughing:

- You are a Materialist Muslim!.

Salem with laughing too:

- No, I am a simple Moslem try to do his business.

Maher with seriously voice:

- You have been not indebted to anybody, We are your brothers...

and continues with laughing:

- We accepted you as what you are, as what you said, just do not forget to let our meetings or any information about us in secret status, do you refuse our friendship?

Faris with shame:

- Thank you very much for your help, and I am proud of your friendship, and I will come back to your future discussion meeting, me too want know who you are?, just give me few future days to reach my work and do some things.

All young-men laughed with high voices, and Faris took leave of them and slunk out.

Maria phoned Mss. Bella to consult her about Mahmoud is offer, and his visa kind that she can not do a public activity, Mss. Bella surprised too, that Mr. Mahmoud who will help her to make a family Christianize meetings for her, but she asked her to wait her soon call-back, she is going to consult Mr. George about!, Maria let her sister wait her decision!, after few hours the call-back became true, George asked her to refuse Mahmoud offer, and she have to contact people lonely in secret, with out Mr. Bobo or his church known, she must work lonely as what he learned her in Milan, and to take her full care!, Maria was nerve that she felt that she need help, this work need assistants, but Mr. George has the knowledge and the power to give the good advice, she decided to go ahead on his advice, wordy, she didn't understood the secret point of Mr. George asking to her to refuse of Mahmoud offer, so she decided to inform her sister about her offer refuse decision!, Sozan found strange of her sister Maria decision, but she has nothing to say, she guessed that her sister project was closed!.

In Milan Mr. George in his office in the Italian intelligence services department thinking about Maria personal mission, he knew her more that herself, he took her file and went to his chef office, he was an old

man uses eyes-glass wore uniform, the two men sat faced each other around empty comfortable table and Maria file between them, George informed his chef about her new news and gave him the file which contain the last report about her, the chef read the report and exchanged this conversation:
Chef:
- In your report you did not wrote your guesses about Mahmoud is offer!.
George:
- She said that he and his wife are don't care about religions!, but she informed Mss. Bella that all the family are praying, and Mahmoud prays –Al-Fager- in the Mosque, so he is a deep-rooted religious, for that I can not believe that deep-rooted Muslim like him can helps Christian to Christianize her people!, this is a mystery!.
Chef:
- But you classed her as a stupid and uncultured .. so you can not trust her ideas, if you do you will be as someone clever follows stupid!, I know that you want to exploit everything for you work, but she will give you a gainsaid information will make you work with hard, specially that she did not knew that she work with an intelligence service, now you must make a scan for all Mahmoud is life to know if he is one of the Libya intelligence agents or no?, forget her and cancel all your connection with her and close her file, that is an order.

George nerve, when he tried to say something, his chef stood up returned back to his desk saying:

- Stop talking George, you make us lose our time.. the Act was done, we don't need a stupid people give us a stupid information, go to you office and carry out my order.

George left-out his chef office with nerve, when he entered his office his phone was rung, Mss. Bella was online, she informed him that Maria did his advice wordy and she will work lonely as what he ordered her!.

Mss. Bella was surprised when George told her that he will not support Maria activities anymore, Mss. Bella tried to ask him to give Maria chance to prove herself, but he refused any new talking about her or her acts and closed the phone.

Mss. Bella were confused too, she felt that she wasn't honest with Maria, She encouraged her to go to Libya and now she failed her, Mr. George act was not a noble doing, how he did that shame?, she knew that he is an intelligence agent, but he was her friend too, he knows that Maria was stupid girl, but she is honest and pure, she deserve a nice treatment!, for that she searches in her mind to find a solution for this problem.

———

(6)
Wolf in the way

Often times Maria has been waking up late, she eats her breakfast in the kitchen lonely, because her sister family awake early, prayed and eat them breakfast with envied energy and happy, she tried to joint them in breakfast but she failed, she kept awake watching TV lonely in her room after midnights, so she awakes lazy in bad mood, but one day next, but that day was differential day, Maria awoke up early, energetic as not her usually, she looked through window to the street, breathed deeply the early dewy air, it was a nice day, through the window she saw trees were filled sparrows song sweet tunes, she perceived the happiness around her, her mind was cleared, and calmed, her feeling was soft and peaceful, felt the safe and felicity sowed in her mind and soul, her body was in good health, as she is in the paradise, she forgot every harms, her long time lonely!, no family!, no friends!, no purpose, her selfish and haughty gone by unknown power as magic, as she was born again without damage to lives new fantastic life!.

Maria never got like that day, she tried to remember but she failed, she did not remember that she was in any time like today, firstly she guessed that the reason of her deep happiness was her body and mind regulated by Libya time zone, but she escaped this idea because she has three weeks, the time zone trouble gone in one week, when she failed to find a reason, she guessed that the lord when he touched her really attend to arise his religion decided to renew her inside, When she reached this point she knelt down and prayed, thanks for the lord.

Maria took a cold shower, its cool felt her a new nice fresh feeling, encouraged her to change some of her style!, usually she has been wearing modest wears, today wanted changing, she had many nice immodest wears bought them along times, she wore some of them shortly in her little past occasions, but she remembered her religion orders!, as a Christian women she ought to wears a modest dresses, as what she done along time, she had bought some immodest dresses for some occasions to be sexy for some people who she wanted to be her future Mr. right, she researched for some one be future husband, but all her efforts failed, all who she found were wanted sex no more, she wanted build a family as every lady been over thirty years old, but she couldn't, she had a nice dreams about her future family as every girls, she lost her dreams ten years ago, then stopped searching, she did not made sex since five years, day after day she lost her looking too, she became did not cared about dresses or body, she been convinced of watching people or TV, watched the life walking far away with her dreams day after day.

The tiring question was:
- Why she brought her immodest dresses to Libya in spite of her known that the Libyans are conservative people?.

She did not found an answer, that she was not guessing that she will search or meet some one to be her husband or boyfriend in Libya!, so she guessed that the lord wanted that for hidden future something!, that thinks led her to esteemed that nice beautiful day the beginning of the future, the day of changing, her inside changed so her outside must be change too.

She heard many times an appear before meant that (Who exploits all his possibilities will be the victorious!), so why she does not exploits all her possibilities to be victor in her secret war against everybody do not been Christian?, but what possibilities she has?, she has not anything, no money, no power, no relations, no friends, she has nothing!, and nothing is not possibility!, she is a poor lady lives her life day per day, no more.

Any way she can wear as she likes in the home, there is no strangers here, she got this justification is enough to wear a new short immodest robe and adorned herself and perfumed with influential perfume, and descended to the kitchen where found her sister family have been around the kitchen table taking them breakfast and talked in funny condition, she seemed differently, nice and fresh, the family invited her to joint them, Beras was amazed for the new Maria immodest style, all of them been more happy for her sharing.

Mahmoud exaggerated for more generosity to her, he stood up and led her to her chair and prepared her coffee with himself laughter, expressed her beauty and her modern style by good and nice words, all the family gladdened her by them nice fancy talking, except Sozan who was sitting silent while she was looking to her with suspected eyes!.

Them welcome and nice talking made Maria felt as a star among her admirers, today the first time her relative Mahmoud expressed her beauty, that act felt her happy and self-confidence, encouraged her to pampered herself with her new admire Mahmoud, Mahmoud exchanged with her some joking about her new look, he was funny, made everybody were been in the kitchen laughed, his clever jokes appeared himself peaceful, Maria thought about her sister loving with him, he was a great man, any lady can love him deeply, she envied her sister who got someone like Mahmoud?, Mahmoud took leave of to his shop, everybody left his seat, Maria mounted stairs to her room to watch TV carried a new coffee.

In that nice fresh day Maria had not known the decision of Mr. George department, Mss. Bella did not informed her to not frustrate her efforts in Tripoli, she have to do the best to one of her church parishs, she has not any international relationship, but anyway she must use all her efforts to succeed Maria efforts by other way.

Maria was full excited to practice all Mr. George order, she must break every limits stand in her holy way, she must be not struggler, does not care about difficulties, even the law limits, but how she can move in secret?, she is not lives lonely, Beras will see her new efforts movements, suddenly she remembered the Swiss man who met him in the airplane!, he asked her to contact him when she will be in Tripoli and need some helps, after short search she found the visit-card of Mr. Bernard Shome which gave to her in the airplane, after few attempts she succeeded to phone him, she was surprised when he remembered her easy!, she had been happy when he welcomed her to her office now if she has a time!, his office address was in the card, after that she phoned Mr. Mohammed the taxi driver to come to her as soon as possible, Mohammed promised her that he will be on the front of her sister home within forty-five minutes, she congratulated herself for this first movement step.

She looked to herself on her wardrobe big mirror, she still beautiful, not as what she was as ten or twenty years ago, but generally she was nice, she pressed her waist to see how it was being in past!, her waist be little fat, her breasts became soft, they lost them stand, advanced her face toward the mirror to inspect its organs, her face still nice too, has some little blond hair, she pulled out them by special tool, then makeup can fix any faults!, she contented with herself, she promised herself to care her body too to be in really a beautiful lady as what Mahmoud described her today.

Now she must make her self ready to her first meeting with that Swiss gentleman, she looked to herself on the mirror and indicated by her forefinger to her mind and her body and told her self with self-confidence:

- My mind and my body Those my two weapons!, my mind will make plans and my body execute, lonely, in secret.

She said that and leant her head to her mirror looked her face nearby thinking, she hoped if Mr. George agreed Mahmoud is help, without any secrecy, did he forgot that she will be lonely?, had no previously experience, Mss. Bella must prays for her mission succeed, she must succeed if compels to sacrifice by everything even self-sacrifice.

Maria did not asked or discussed with herself that everybody has mind like her, most of them not good people like her sister family and her good neighbors, some people has the Satan experience!.

Maria decided to use all her weapons to impress Mr. Shome, all her weapons must use in her future war as what she named her person mission, even female weapon, truly her religion forbad this way, but she gave herself a false explanation, that Christ lived before many very old centuries were people were simple and pure, everything was clear, now the life became complicated and swarming, everybody wants be the first one, so she must take the short way to get the win, if Mr. George order her to work lonely and in secret, she must do the best, and she had not other way to apply his order, she had not knowing that Mr. George did that because he was one of intelligence agents and he wanted made her one of them agents!, she felt that her new explanation is true!, forgot the simple saying which mean: by evil way you can't get the goodness!, she thought consult Mss. Bella but she do not want lose more time, she guessed that Mss. Bella as one of the old Christian style, maybe has and old viewpoints, then she must do the best by new simple way.

She defined her goal, that who is to get the friendship of Mr. Shome by short way, she guessed that he has some possibilities can she uses to do something, if she can changes the religion of one Libyan to be

Christian she will considers herself been win, she must use the classic simple female way, female when she wants something from Male, the old life rule-examined way by females along the history.

Mr. Shome must help her to serve her lord, he must be in her side, she guessed that he will be her friend in Libya if she will make him loves her, so she must do all what she can doing to get his attention.

Maria hurried to practice her idea, for that she wore a short skirt showed her upside thighs and narrow blouse showed a large part of her breasts and red foothold shoes to arise and lengthen her blond legs, and adorned her face and hair, Sozan came to her sister to ask her about her last phones, she knocked the door and opened it, she amazed when found her sister prepare herself to go out!, Maria did not cared about his sister inquiry silence looking, but when she asked her:

- Where you are going as a whore?.

Maria replies with calm voice while she prepares herself:

- This is not your business!.

Salma was in the salon with Azza who came early to go together with Salma to the market, but they heard the voice of Souzan came from up stairs they hurried up mounted the stairs, the two sons came in the front of the room followed them mother voice too, all of them looking too to Maria new style, Salma and her brothers laughed in secret while they were exchanged meaning looks, Azza as a riotous one whistled a long admiration whistle, which let everybody there laughed

highly, even Maria too, who turned her face to Azza and thanked her with laughing, Azza told her:
- Oh my god .. you are very sexy, as a star!.
Maria bent her head to Azza laughing and said:
- Thank you Azza, kindly come in.
Azza and Salma entered the room while others divided far as just as he was been.
Azza and Salma re made her makeup and her looking, Azza asked Maria with wink laughter:
- Who is the lucky man will meet this sexy lady?.
Maria hugged Azza and laughter, Azza can not controlled her self, she kissed her lips deeply and long, Salma surprised that her aunt reacted to Azza kissing her with appetite, which led her to poke them deeply to separate them, the two Misses stood up been panted and laughter, while Salma screamed saying:
- Are you crazies? .. oh god .. what are you doing?.
Maria replied her:
- What?, do you be jealous of me to your friend?, she is my friend too.
Azza smiled and completed the last touches to make Maria be fantastic lady, then Azza looked her carefully and re whistled again, then Maria jumped to hug her again Salma jumped too among them her hands to let them far of each others directed to her aunt warned her saying:
- Stop, you will spoil your makeup again!.
Maria stopped and replied her laughter:
- Is this an advice or jealousy?.
Salma kissed her aunt front saying with laughter too:
- Both!.

She said that and took hold of her aunt shoulders looked in her eyes saying with full feeling:
- My lovely aunt I am happy for your happiness.

Salma act changed Maria from joke to high feeling, this is the first time she looked the deep of Salma eyes, they were beautiful and clear, among soft beautiful face, Maria hugged Salma whispered in her ear by too low voice:
- Really thank you Salma, Kindly you are good family, I am proud of you, and I am sorry for everything bad I done or said .. please take my apology to all the family .. do you promise me? .. please do that for me! .. do you?.

Maria said that with silent cry, and repeated her asking many times, did not stopped just when she heard Salma promised her, Azza looked them sad statuses, then she screamed for them saying:
- Oh .. oh .. save your sad feeling to other time .. Maria you spoiled your makeup again!.

Azza said that and separated them with some force, laughter, the two girls dried them eyes by tissues, Azza by her clever jokes made them laughed again, and the two girls fixed Maria makeup again, Maria was happy for them clever help, and lovely feeling.

When Maria been readied they heard The taxi piping, they appeared to him through the window, Maria took her hand sac and kissed her friends and took leave to go, the two girls asked her to take care, and hoped a nice time for her, Maria left them, they closed her room and descended down to salon.

Sozan was in salon when Maria went out, she smiled and said bye-bye for her, the two girls noted Sozan is sad been, for that they rounded her and tried to make her laugh, Sozan smiled for them and left them to the kitchen.

Sozan was too sad, her sister behavior is too bad, she did not care about her behavior in the house with her family, but when she wears an shameful dresses and wanders in Tripoli streets often she will put herself in troubles!, also her quarter families are shamed people, don't like women wear shameful dresses to save them adolescents, for that she did her domestic doing without concentration while Azza and Salma went to Market.

Mohammed carried Maria to the address looking in secret to Maria naked legs and breasts with shock, he does not understood her new behavior, in Barnouss home in the first meeting she seemed as an old-fashioned person, but today she been different, when he reached the address, which was in nice place, in end of walk-way, some far from the drive road, so he indicated her the building door, Maria asked him to be ready to carry her back, and left the car walked to the place, Maria sensed the walkers looking to her, and heard some whistles, she felt her glory, but she felt down when someone walked beside her and said by Arabic language something which she does not know, when he guessed that she is not a Libyan he said by bad English language laughter (hello whore! .. how much is your price?), Maria did not turned to him, she had feared the fall down, but she walked away hurried!, prays in herself to the god to save her from public, this is the second time she hears the word (whore) today by two languages!, finely she reached the building in safe.

When entered the company floor and represented herself to the reception desk, she amazed when the security led her to an empty room and inspected her and her sac deeply, that felt her down shortly, and they led her to Mr. Shome office who been stood in his door space waiting her with amaze smile too!.

Mr. Shome was an old, tall, clever person, hide her deception behind soft behavior and large smiles, he was an arduous man, but with softly which everybody could not knew his reality, he was a human wolf.

Mr. Shome was been waiting other person kind, he saw Maria in the airplane and in Tripoli airport who she was modest, and enthusiastic religious, now he has been looking for a lady comes directly naked to him!, he controlled his surprised behind high welcoming talks.

He shook hands with her and bent kissing her hand and welcomed her to enter his special office and sat her in comfortable couch been in her large modern office, inspected her breasts and naked legs by greedy eyes.

He sat facing her continues his desire looks to her naked body and he try to foresees the really reason for her visit!, he know that in the first visit people be carefully, specially ladies, he created a view about her character, but with her new looking she broke his previous knowledge, how are she?, is she a coy

Christian religious?, or an easy lady?, why she came as naked through coy people?, and is she usually wears shameless dresses or just today special for him?, if she came as naked special for his meeting, so what is her really purpose?, his little information about her did not support him to foretell for her visit goal, but in generally he guessed that she came to put him in her pocket.

Mr. Shome has two welcoming kinds, one officially, in order to use a dark tray contents thermos of coffee, tea, and cold water, other welcome kind for special occasional meeting where he use the white hidden tray contents bottles of different alcohol drinks, ice pieces vessel, and some cheese.

In order of this special personal occasion he chose the hidden white tray for her reception, so he stood up and brought the hidden white tray and put it on the small salon table apposite to her, then he took his seat faced to her went too far in her blond naked legs beauty with full appetite saying with fluent Italian language:

- I am happy that a nice lady like you can share with a lonely man like me a cup of drink!.

He said that and filled up two cups from one bottle with some pieces of ice and gave her one with laughter.

Maria felt up that she had long time did not heard one single word of man praises her beauty or shares drink with her or see with appetite her female body .. she felt that she lives a really happy time, she extended her hand to catch the cup while laughter and said with spoil voice:

- I have the honor to be that lady.

She said that and drank some of her cup, it was a cup of whisky.

Mr. Shome continues his appetite looking to her showed body, while Maria embezzles looking to him with pleasure and relaxation pretend scrutinized the office furniture.

His craving looks cautioned her that this nice gentleman is dangerous, he is not as what she thought, she saw this desire looks before, it is looks of men want make sex no more, she closed that door since ten years ago, she need his sympathy to help her, but her naked made his full attention for her body, she repented of her doing, her shameful dresses wearing, the words (whore) by Italian language from Sozan, and by English language from that rascal passer-by, sounding in her inside, she is not a whore!, she is a good person, she felt that she lost the proof of her goodness, now she is sitting apposite this unknown wolf man naked, drinking alcohol!, does she became crazy?, how she came with this dirty looking to an unknown man for first time meeting wants his respect?, her repentance made her body trembled, she became as some one wake up suddenly!, why her mind was not leading her to the right way?, she was wrong and she must correct her mistake.

Mr. Shome noted her shaking, he did not guessed her new idea change, his appetite led him to be away, he just thought that she is as ready food came with itself to him, she came by herself to be in his hold without asking, she readied her self to be eaten, he don't know yet her reason!, but he will, he is a good hunter, he knows how and when toward or backward, how he can make the fish come easy into his net, if she came to him today with different face, so her intend became different too, he decided to eat her now, his experience led him to do that now, if he can not forward his position to eat her now he will find some difficulties in the future, this is his chance to pleasure himself, and to include her to his victims set.

For that Mr. Shome encouraged her to complete drinks her cup, he know that the drink will relaxes her to be easy to joint his net, Maria attended for his hidden purpose, she said seriously laughter:
- Thank you Mr. Shome for you kindly welcoming .. really I am happy to meet a gentleman like you, about drink .. I have not been imagining to drink alcohol in Libya!, even in Italy I had not drunk alcohol .. I will drink just this cup with you!.

Her seriously accent worried Mr. Shome, he is lonely in Libya where no whores can taken easy of his sexual need, for that this is an un-anticipated chance for him to enjoy himself, he think that hunt will gone, he amazed for her quick change!, he gulped down his spittle with heard sound and said:
- Oh dear .. I am sorry .. I guessed that you need some alcohol cups .. but no problem I have wine .. we can drink wine!.

He said that and went to his chest and brought a bottle of wine, but Maria with laughing voice said:
- No .. no Mr. shone .. please .. I am not here to drink wine .. please sit-down.

But Mr. Shome sat beside her closely showed her the old date of the wine which wrote on the bottle article, Maria moved her sitting to be some far from him, but Mr. Shome moved his body too to be adjacent her, she felt his warm breaths on her neck, which made her heart throbs been quick and tremor flood her body, she felt that she will dissolve in his hug, she found difficult to controlled herself but she stood up laughed saying:

- Ok Mr. Shome .. I have to leave.

Mr. Shome with laughter catches her hand try to seat her on his thighs, but her withstood freed her hand, then he stood and tried to hug her but Maria gathered her force and pushed him back saying screamily:

- No .. no .. please .. you are civilized person!, please let me go!.

Mr. Shome stood un-believed that his hunt will gone, he stopped laugh saying:

- Just for some pleasure .. I loved your body!.

Maria became completely angry, she took her hand-sac and went to the door, Mr. Shome preceded her to the closed door stood in Maria way saying:

- What do you do?, I am not a wild man!.. please wait!.

Maria stopped her walk looking for him with higher saying:

- Really you are a wild man! .. but do not worry .. just let me go!.

Mr. Shome said seriously this time:

- You came to me as naked, you excited me .. I am a man!.

Maria said with nerve:

- Ok .. I am sorry .. just let me leave!.

Mr. Shame smiled to her and extended his hand to shake hands with her saying:

- Friends!.

Maria laughed saying:

- Friends!.

Mr. Shome laughter and said:

- Ok .. if we became friends, let my driver carries you to your home!.

Maria become glad, because she don't wants walks again in the street. Then she shook his hands saying:

- Yes please .. and thank you again.

Mr. Shome gave her two bottles of wine in dark sac as gift and called for his driver who came quickly, Maria left him with smiling following the driver to the exit door.

Sozan was in the front home watered them small garden, stood with Azza and Salma when a large car stopped apposite her house, the driver opened the right back door and led out Maria, he gave her sacs and left her away.

Maria with the girls amazed about The strange car and Maria seat in the right back chair as a minister, Sozan noted the name of the company which wrote on the front doors, the ladies welcomed her, Sozan become fine when she saw her sister in safe, but she worried for her new secret connection with this company too, Maria shook hands with them laughing, and held Azza is hand and asked her to enter the home with her, Azza entered with her while Salma stayed to help her mother.

In the room the two girls exchanged some joking with high laughing as what Maria English language possible, Azza helped Maria to takeoff one's clothes, and asked her about her new black sac contents, Maria showed her the wine bottles, and asked her to keep that in secret, Azza did not experienced the drink before so she asked Maria for one cup of wine, but Maria warned her about the smell, for that they delayed the drink to other suitable time.

----

(7)
Happens in the same time

* *Maria movement in that day led Souzan to guess that Maria planned to go ahead to Christianize Libyan lonely in secret, maybe her group in Milan ordered her to do that in secret, or she decided that with herself, anyway her decision will reaction to her family law invitation, she wants know the relation reason between her sister and the company who carried her to home by stately car, which indicates to that her relation was with a Manager in the company who can order to carry her with stately car, she wrote the company name and its information in a paper and gave it to Mahmoud to investigate about the company and its Manager, without any question!, Mahmoud worried but he promised her to do that as possible as soon, he guessed that Sozan gathers information about her sister!. * Sozan thought to cancel her sister visa and send her back to Italy, she seemed in her imagine that she is a danger one, she is not easy person, but her sisterly sentiment prevented her.*

* *Some of Mahmoud males neighbors who saw the naked of Maria in that morning talking together about her shameless dress and informed Masjed Imam about her doing and asked him to talk with Mr. Mahmoud to fix his relative behavior.*

* *Some of Mahmoud females neighbors decided to go together to Sozan to know the reason of her sister shameless dresses wearing!.*

Azza thinking to make a relationship with Maria and voyage with her to Italy when she return back, she asked Maria to be in her company to church, she wants know the inside contents of Church, Maria happy for her asking, she deemed is a chance to talk with her about the Christianity, but because her English language is little, so Mr. Bobo will help her, and Salma asked Azza to go with them after her mother (Sozan) consultation.

** Maria congratulated herself that she succeeded in her first goal which was connect a friendship relation with Mr. Shome, after she had corrected her shameless mistake, she looking for the future to enlarge it as possible as soon, and thinking to receive the Gospels books from the church and invite Azza, Barnous and any of who was not religious to change them religion to be Christians!.*

** Mr. Shome decided to make relationship with Maria but under his rules, he needs her body from time to time when he is in Libya and for some of his other hidden business, as what he said to himself that not usually he can find an easy crazy lady!.*

** Faris began her new work easy and he tries to know his new job.*

** Salem and his band observing the quarter people, note everything and some targets as Mr. Faris.*

** Two different Extremes Muslims bands changed them home meeting to the quarter.*

** Unknown someone thrust Barnous home by fired bottles but no big damages, the police interrogated people, and Barnouss rejoiced when heard about Maria shameless dress worn, the parents* ordered them daughters to be near Maria and serve her.

* Mr. Bobo thinking about what Maria can do if she has a good position, he decided to support Maria as possible if she is going to spread out the Christianity in Libya!.

* Police station detectives in the quarter watching and listing all quarter rudder movements.

* Mss. Farida bought a new small clinic in the quarter, she equipping it with new clinical materials and she is going to opening it soon.

* In Milan Mss. Bella found someone Italian religious works with an Italian company in Libya promised her to support Maria in her holy doing in Libya, but she did not know that he is one of Mr. George agents in Tripoli, Mrs. George puts him in her searching way to follow Maria doings in Tripoli.

* In Milan Mr. George tries to persuade his administration to enlarge his activity in Libya and give him more authorities, and behind his administration he ordered one of his agent in Tripoli to send him the last Maria news.

* Mohammed, the Taxi driver became suspected to Maria affairs.

* Mahmoud and his two sons listened to some bad rumors about them family, people didn't liked them relative Maria behaves, people will interrupt them if Maria will go on in her shameless behavior!.

* Mahmoud going to Check his guard cameras memory daily, to know what happened around his house.

* Fatma and many friends neighbors worried too about Mahmoud family new bad repute.

* Sami, the quarter homes maintenances technician who was a friend of Mahmoud sons from young time loves them sister Salma in secret since many years, he decided in the end to send to her the first love letter behind her brothers knowing.

* some one watching the church from on facing tall tree.

* Masjed Imam received a menace letter from unknown to practice the Islam law for Barnous family who described them as unbelievers, and everybody do not prays in the Masjed, and gather charities to poor families, Masjed Imam gave the letter to the police station.

* Some of police men inspected the quarter coffee which found a medium quantity of drug, they arrested the coffee owner.

* Police car chased an unknown car carried four persons but the unknown car fired them and gone.

* Large demonstration in Tripoli center for freedom and justice to Philistine people against Israel expanded politics on Philistine land and them new massacres in Ghazza.

* Some of young men musicians volunteered to give life amusing music soirees to the families in the quarter square, hot dialog in Masjed about some people want separate females and males, others don't want music soirees at all, Masjed Imam wants satisfy all, but he couldn't.

―――――

(8)

Strangers bring Troubles

On Sunday morning the three girls entered the church main hall through its open door, Maria asked her two friends with low voice to sit in back and she jointed the prayers, Mr. Bobo was on the stage with the songsters saw everything, he amazed and be glad in same time about Azza and Salma coming with Maria, he knows that they are not Christians.

Azza and Salma sat in them seats with turning heads scrutinized the interior church ornamentation and tried to know the pray words which was with an old unknown language.

After the praying Mr. Bobo and the church nun and monk came together to welcome Azza and Salma, some of prayers came too, many of them know Salma and Azza, they were working in the Market, coiffeurs, bakeries, bathrooms, and many of other places in the quarter, Maria introduced her two friends for all as the new Libyan Christians!, for that many of them surprised and glad too for this new news, Azza and Salma laughed but they did not made any reactions about Maria introduce, Mr. Bobo toured with them in the Church parts explained everything for them with smiles, Azza asked him many questions, but Salma just watching, after the tour Mr. Bobo and his Church colleagues invited them with Maria to drink something in the church office salon, Mr. Bobo did not esteemed

Maria first meeting introduce was really, He knows that Salma was her niece, but he don't know Azza who seemed for him as a riotous girl, his colleagues think that is really that this two girls a new Christians, for that they were too enthusiastic, for that in the office salon some misunderstand conversation been.

The Church salon was too large and comfort all of them sat in his place watching others, but most attention was to Maria and her Libyan friends who sat beside themselves. The Nun distributed sweets and fruit juice cups for all who was been there, The Monk was the first talker. Asking Azza with Arabic who was the many asking one:

The Monk:

- Mss. Azza why you want be a Christian one?.

Azza looked to Maria and smile to remember her as some one asking help in side and in other side she don't want say something will reaction to Maria, Maria noted her help look, so she asked Mr. Bobo to let the monk speak English with slowly, Mr. Bobo translated to her the monk question to Azza, Maria did no said anything to avoid the misunderstand, Azza was embarrassed, but with some difficult she replied with shame smile and frankly:

- I am not!.

The monk amazed, but he smiles and looks to Maria inquiring, Mr. Bobo asked him to speak English because Maria she don't understand Arabic, so The monk translated what she replied with laughing, all who were been there looked to Maria to understand!, but Maria still silenced smiled which encouraged Salma to explained the truth:

- Look Mr. monk, Mss. Maria is my aunt and Azza is my friend, we came with her today to visit the church to see the inside parts, but we did not came to discuss the religions!... we are a normal visitors as a friends .. no more!.

The monk guessed that there is some joking included, for that he laughed and said with doubt:
- Ok .. you welcome as a secret Christians!.

Salma and Azza exchanged a meaning looks with silent, Mr. Bobo with Maria left the office for short time and Maria came back with a big yellow envelope contents the Arabic Gospels copies, Azza and Salma took leave of everybody and followed Maria who walked slowly with Mr. Bobo talking with whispering to the church door.

In the return back way Maria gave Azza one Gospel copy, Azza took it with thanks, but Azza changed some of her thinks about Maria, she seemed for her as mystery!, she don't care about her friends or everybody, because she did not explained anything about her introducing to the church people which made misunderstand, while she sat with crazy smile, and she is religious one wants publishing her religion anyway in time of dressing shameless dresses, and kissing her lips with appetite!, she wants her friendship but she hates every religious and irregular people.

Salma did not commented about her aunt behaves, she asked Azza to don't care and smiled.

On the advertisements board on quarter public hall facing they found the soirees music advertisement, they been glad, on the back way Maria asked Azza and Salma to combine her to do a short visit to Barnous *family but Salma refused her asking and forced Azza to be with her, then they waited her in the street after Barnous house behind some trees while Maria visited Barnous Family shortly on the door step and gave them three copies of Gospel and left them with promised to return to them in next future days.*

In that afternoon all Christians in the quarter spread a rumor with glory, talked that Mss. Maria the Italian Christian encouraged Mss. Salma and Mss. Azza to be Christians too, and they changed them religions in the church today morning.

When Salma in home talking with her mother about her visiting to the church and what happened, the door bell knocked when Sozan opened the door she found nobody there but she found an letter envelope staked on the door out face, the envelope was addressed to Mss. Salma, Sozan brought the envelope with amazed and gave it to Salma who amazed too.

Salma opened the envelope and read an included letter, when finished she laughed highly and gave it back to her mother, it was a letter from Sami the technician informed her with nice words that he has been loving her since long time, as a nice serious girl, his shame stopped him to show her his feeling and also he was not ready for marriage, he asked to forgive him if he made any mistake but he wants know her regard because he wants married her as possible as she wants, and finally asked her to keep this letter in secret if he don't wants him for any reason and don't knowledge her brothers or fathers who respected them deeply and do not misunderstand him at all.

Sozan gave back to Salma the letter and sat on one of the salon chair slowly, Salma re read the letter many times with thinking, and looked to her mother to know what she must do, Sozan looked to her son with love, she remembered the first love letter she received when she was student from her colleague, she in same position of her daughter now, surprised and happy in same time, she controlled herself and said with low voice to her:

- Listen to me Salma .. take this letter seriously, Sami is a good Youngman, we knew him long time ago, give yourself a chance, keep this letter in secret, we will invite him and you can talk with him .. he is a serious person, if you can loved him as he was .. then every thing will be alright .. if no you can frankly to him and give him back his letter.

Salma look down few minutes and said:

- Yes Mom .. he is a good Youngman .. but never I felt that he looked to me as a lover, I respect him but I did not thought about him as a lover .. really I am confusing.

Sozan said with laugh to lighten her confuse:

- If you have not a certain lover as what I know .. this is a chance for you from a known young gentleman, serious and ashamed, loving you too much, and ready for marriage .. meet him .. you have nothing to lose.

Salma felt herself fined, she smiled and went to her mother, the two ladies fell in huge hug laughing.

In the night most quarter families went to the square to show to music soiree, all the place was clean the colored lights made the place with the big garden shone, they organized the place to be in the front opposite the platform the tables with chairs for families and chairs in the back for singles, every neighbors been together, girls, boys, ladies, men, young men, in groups, talking, exchanging jokes and listening in same time, some of young men dancing in the back, they ashamed to dance facing ladies, some girls dancing facing all, the Barnous sisters mounted the platform with the singers and danced.

Maria was with Azza and Salma and some other girls, she did not understand the songs language but she dance over the music, suddenly they showed her on the platform dancing with Barnous sisters, Maria was not a good dancer but the two Barnouss sisters was as a professional dancers, all of the quarter people amazed for them even them enemies, Azza has not the courage to follow Maria, she wants to mount the platform, but she feared the anger of her brother Faris, for that she stood waves to Maria and Barnouss, Salma rounded her head searching to see Sami who was behind her with her two brothers, he guessed that she searching for him, for that he went to beside her were she can see him, he was happy when he saw her smile to him, but to not alertness her brother he returned back sat with them, Mahmoud spent some time in the soiree with some men and left back to his home to take some rest.

After few time some one screamed from the back side cursed all of people been there, he screamed that the music and dance will anger Allah, but some young-men drove him away.

In that night through the soiree behind of Bera family partners and them known friends hearing the people exchanged the rumor talk about Salma and Azza baptism by Maria in the church, as what some Christians said, Sami heard that rumor, he denied it and chided who talked that, but he worried, he look to Salma from far perhaps to look to him side, she did from time to time and smile to him, he sighs for her meeting to know the reality.

Fatma and some of Beras friends denied the Christianize rumor too, not because they knew the truth but because they trusted Beras at all, but the people still have some misunderstand.

Faris and some religious young men ashamed to go to the music soiree with them family, they went to the coffee who its owner in the prison, it was empty, just some people here or there, smoking (shisha) or playing (Nard), or watching TV, the music echo come from far away through the quiet night with its cold breeze.

Faris noted some new bearded faces in the coffee, some of them had a long beard, for that he asked some friends about them, they informed him that they are new rudder, but because he had a long time did not came to coffee he did not met them, Faris approached to one of them who was stood up near the bar and asked him with smile:
- Salamou Alaikom!. (hello).

The bearded man looked to Faris slowly with care and replied (Assalam) (hello) with unwanted voice and act, and returned his face to the other side, but Faris did not hopeless, so he asked him again:
- How are you? .. I am Faris lives here!.

The man saw for him again and replied with stony face:
- Are you living here?.

Faris with laugh and elongated his hand to shake hands, but the man did not longed his hand, Faris been ashamed and returned his hand back beside his body, and answered his question:
- Yes .. I am living here!.

The man continued:
- Are you a Muslim?.

Faris amazed for his question meaning, but he said with patient:
- Yes, I am a Muslim!.

The strange man:
- You are a Muslim and your family females in the evil music soiree, the Satan meeting, dancing with strangers!.

Faris surprised for the acts and talking of him, but he controlled his self and said with a calm voice:
- Where is the Satan meeting?.. All quarter family are there no one stranger, no evil there!, there is just the quarter families going to get some fun!.

The bearded man screamed with nerve:
- Some fun! .. Some fun!.. forbidden fun .. men and women together as animals for fun! .. fun leads to sin!.. sin leads to hell! .. you are not a Muslim!.. you are not a man!.. go away!.

All who were in the coffee turned them heads looking and hearing them, Faris be nerves too, he looked around for everybody attention to his reaction for the bearded insult, but he controlled himself and went back to his friends seats silent, his friends blamed hem for his talking with like this stony excessive people, his friends had a good deep Islam culture, they can discuss him, but this people kinds does not discuss any subject without nerve, and they will insult them discussion part, that act made anybody does not like discuss them by anyway.

Someone bearded came to Faris and his friends table, asking them to talk!, the young-men welcomed him, the man sat on nearly chair and introduced himself as: Mr. Farhat, a new abode in the quarter, a biology teacher in center Tripoli school, after that he said directed his talk to Faris:

- We are some Muslims young-men group, I came here to inform you our admire, we liked yourself controlling, The messenger of Allah Mohamed (God's blessing and peace be upon him) said:

- (The believer in Allah does not defames, does not courses, does not say obscene or dirty.)and said in other position said:

- (The strong man is not who can throw down people!, The strong man who controlling himself in anger!), you are really a good Muslim!.

Faris been shied, he thanked the man and said with ashamed voice:

- Brother do not exaggerate my doing, I am not a good or perfect Muslim, The Islam perfection is as a large river, pure and clear, every Muslim could seize what he can load for himself, but human is weak, some human look for the outside of doings, others have deep view see for the inside of doings, Islam is the religion of human nature, The messenger of Allah Mohamed (God's blessing and peace be upon him) said:

- (amuse yourselves from time to time, the hearts become weary like bodies!.).

And in other position sad:

- (I am a human, fast and break the fast, sleep and awake, marry the woman, everybody did not do like my doings is not mine!).

and in other places:

- (The Islam is too deep, navigate in it slowly).

And:

- (look-out for the excessive!).

And:

- (the excess is as the minus).

In the true Sunna he carried his wife Aicha on his shoulder to see the Negro funny playing facing his home, this is the Islam which we knew, simply, easy, practically, affectionate, peaceful, satisfy the human needs.

Mr. Farhat listened to Faris word by word with full attention, when Faris finished his talk he smiled and said:

- Yes .. that is true, Islam a human life system made by Allah, the unlimited force who created the cosmos, humans, and the life, Humans are limited things could not know over them limitation, for that the messenger ordered Muslims to navigate in Islam slowly, .. it is easy and difficult in same time .. thank you Mr. Faris.

The young men continued talking about the easy Islam for the easy life, after few time, Faris and his friends talked frankly with Farhat that they thought that he is an excessive person cause of his beard, Farhat laughed and amazed for them frankly, Farhat jointed his friends with Faris friends, became a large of regulated or balanced Muslims group as most of Muslims worldwide.

Next day, Sozan received some of her female neighbors who came to her enquiring about, them relation with Barnouss and her sister shameless dresses behavior and Salma and Azza Christianized, Sozan esteemed that is a chance to family defense against any rumors, Sozan explained every what was happened, about Barnouss, and Salma and her friend Azza in the church, the two girls went with Maria just to see inside of the church not for any other purpose, and she undertook for them for Maria to not dress any shameless dresses out of her house in the future, the ladies promised Sozan to be her family friends as they were in the past and they will inform everybody the truth, The men neighbors went to Mahmoud in his shop and talked with him about the three subjects, his talked is nearly of Sozan talked, the men promised him too.

Sozan and Mahmoud thanked Allah for that, and they were decided to talk with Maria about everything with large frankly to not replay the story again.

Mahmoud and Sozan informed Maria about the bad rumors about them and asked her that she must not dress any shameless dresses outside the house and do not carry any Muslim companion to the church, in the beginning Maria become tigerish but in the end she submitted to them asking.

Fatma also did the same act for her daughter Azza, all of the two families relied on the time for people to be silent.

A day next, Sozan and Salma made a date with Sami in an nice calm coffee beside the sea beach far of the quarter, at afternoon of the day to talk about his letter, Salma was very happy waiting the afternoon by empty patience, thinking about her first date with a really lover, who chose her from hundreds girls in the quarter, she felt that she been glory and distinct, looking for herself on mirror and check her suitable robes time to time sameness, she was happy and confused, this was the first time she thought about a man as a lover, her lover, special for her for ever, he and she were virgin, no one stranger touched them interior bodies, she remembered The holy Koran speaking:

- (The good men for the good women).

Her eyes shed some tears, she sensed that she was in critical point in her life history, does she found in his deep character and culture a space for her hope to live her future life close and open in same time as her great father and mother, is his love to her a key to future happy life?, is he a regulated Muslim man not an extreme one knows the Islam as a jail and he is the jailer?, she wants him as her father, and she will be as her mother, is he suitable for her and her think?, or he loved her outer?, every this ideas details will be known after this critical date.

Mr. Shome phoned Maria to meet her, Maria invited him to come to her home in afternoon to spend some time together, his driver indicated him to the home, in afternoon Maria was with him in the salon lonely, where nobody in home, she received him dressed a short robe with nice make-up, brought one of the two wine bottles with some ice and filled up a cup for him and put the tray above the salon table, Mr.

Shome pleased with the empty home, for that he enjoyed himself, Maria played a slow Italian music, Mr. Shome drank some cups of wine and sat opposite to her smiles, did not said anything, Maria sat on her settee looking for him smiles too, suddenly the door bell knocked, Maria saw Azza in the door by the cameras TV, at outset she did not wanted to open the door for her, but she remembered that Azza did not speak Italian, then she opened the door for her smiles with large welcoming and she introduced her to Mr. Shome, who took that as a chance to know a Libyan girl, Azza saw the wine bottle on the table so she embraced Maria as she fights her with screamed joking:

- This is a big treason .. you promised give me some wine cups but you didn't, you drank the bottle alone with your friend.

Mr. Shome amazed for Azza gut, he had not any previous dealing with Libyan females, that is his first time met a Libyan girl in her nature environment, Azza gleeful pleased him, Maria was pleased too, tried to self-defend by screamed saying too:

- No .. no dear .. I am not traitorous .. I saved your bottle yet!.

Azza laughed highly looked to Mr. Shome and said:

- So .. this is your hidden friend .. who gave you the wine bottles:

Mr. Shome replied with English language with laugh too:

- I am not a hidden! .. I well present some wine to you too .. we are friends now!.

Azza said frankly:
- I will not wait your future presents .. I will drink some cups now!.

She said that and filled the two cups of wine and drunk them shortly she drank two other cups, which propelled Maria to take away the bottle out her reach, and she sat back on near settee panting, Maria and Mr. Shome laughed about her comedy act.

Mr. Shome asked Azza with some worry:
- Are you ok? .. if this is the first time you drink so it is enough for you!.

Azza felt ecstasy flowed in her veins changed her mood, colors be more shines with some beautiful mixed up, she saw to Mr. Shome and laughed highly saying:
- It is not enough!.. but I will stop because my mother will kill me if she senses for my drunk .. we are as slaves here .. parents .. neighbors .. brothers .. community .. all of them controlling us!.

Maria and Shome pleased for her frankly talking, each one from his viewpoint side, Maria was in her seat, her short robe waned back showed her yellow underpants, Azza looked to Maria and laughed highly referring to her underpants saying:
- Your yellow underpants is beautiful Maria .. I love it!.

Maria embarrassed, she merged her legs quickly as she was stinging and said laughing ashamed:
- Oh .. Azza .. Do you be drunk?.

Mr. Shome screamed laughed deeply, shared Azza her drunk joking said through his laughing indicated to Maria closed legs too:
- And her underpants loves you too.. Azza!.

Azza laughed too much deeply, her breath on the point of stop, Mr. Shome took it as a chance for more sexy fun, then suddenly he took high the down end of Azza robe showing her blonde legs and her underpants which was yellow too, so he said highly with deep laughing:

- Oh .. Azza your underpants is yellow too, Azza did not worried of his act or covered again her down body, she continuous her laughing try to control her self looking to Mr. Shome and saying screamily:

- I think your underpants is yellow too Mr. Shome!.

Mr. Shome went ahead sharing her jokes, he stood up and took down his pantaloons to show her his underpants which was red, Azza looked to his underpants and said with slowly voice:

- Look at!.. it is yellow!.

Maria been nerve, but she don't wants spoiling her two rash friends fun time, she shared them fun saying to Azza:

- Are you blinded? .. it is red!.

Azza by her uncontrollable character and the wine be her rash one more, she signaled to him to be close, when he became close to her she elongate her hand with gut and handled his cock which been stood up under her fingers and said with highly laughing:

- Yes Maria it is red .. It is dangerous!.

All of them laughed deeply them breathes been intermittent and them eyes filled with tears, Maria stood up and slapped Mr. Shone on his rear to wear his pantaloons and led down Azza robe to cover her legs, Azza controlled herself and sat well in her seat dry up her eyes, she felt her head became heavy but she still in good mood, everybody returned to his seat trying to control himself and dry his eyes.

Maria took leave from Mr. Shome to carry Azza to her room in up stairs, Azza went with her stumbled, She lay her on the bed and asked her to be quite and get sleep to flow out her drunk.

When Sozan and Salma entered the coffee, the place of the date, they saw Sami sat apposite a table far of others, they went to him smiled, Sami welcomed them while he looking to Salma who was very beautiful in her nice long blue robe, Sozan sat with them few minutes and took leave to sat in other table near them to let them alone, she said that and changed her place to far table.

Sami and Salma was to ashamed looking far of each other, but after few time Salma controlled her ashamed then look to Sami and said with low voice calm voice:

- Sami I want ask you some questions needs clear and honest answers!.

Sami gathered himself dispersions and looked to Salma saying seriously:

- Yes Salma, ask me for everything you want!.

Salma:

- Firstly, why you loved me from long time as what you said in your letter?.

Sami swallowed his saliva with heard noise which propelled Salma to laugh shortly which confused him, but he smiled to Salma and said with ashamed voice:

- I am sorry Salma .. this is the first time that I met a girl lonely, specially you ..yes Salma specially you ..

you are my dream-girl since when I grew up .. Why? .. you want know why? .. ok .. as you know that I am a friend of your brothers since our young, I saw you everyday often, never I saw you or heard that you did a shame or bad doing, for that I loved you as a good girl.

Salma been happy and been down too, because he did not talked about her femininity, but Sami attended for his forgot so he continued quickly:
- And your beauty too, I saw you the most beautiful girl in the world.

When he said that Salma became in high feeling, sensed herself swim on the clouds, she did not controlled her self so she put her two hands on his hands, and she back to reality when Sami backward his hands, Salma returned back her hands too with some ashamed, but she controlled herself again and asked him with serious voice:
- How you can imagine the marriage life?.

Sami with laughing said:
- I am a normal man, regulated religious as your father and brothers and Faris, I felt that I have to live my life with easy and activity to build a small good family with a good female partner.

Salma informed Sami about her visiting to the church and her aunt joking presentation to the Christians in church that she and her friend Azza were a new Christians, but that is not a true, the true was they were visited the church just to know its inside parts as a curiosity point no more, Sami pleased for her frankly, he believed her story deeply.

The Youngman informed her that he built a small flat on his family home which been far of two streets from her home, and he furnished his flat with every home needs, he seemed to her as someone made the necessary bases for new born family.

Sami was as what Salma wanted and liked, she thanked Allah who sent to her this pure Youngman lover, but she had not given him her end word, she told him that she will inform her males family to give him the end word, and she gave him back his letter, she said that and called her mother to leave, while Sami sat in his seat fills his eyes with her soft beauty.

Maria spent some more fun time with Mr. Shome while Azza slipped in her room, Mr. Shome forced her with joking to kiss her, Maria resisted his violence joking but in the end she gave him some long kisses and hugs.

When Salma and Sozan returned back to them home Maria was in her room lay beside her sleeper friend Azza looking to roof and thinking, the effects of kissing still been.

Souzan saw Azza lay on the bed when she review Maria in her room, Maria explained Azza sleeping cause, that she felt headache, Salma run to her friend to see what she has been happening?, she bowed down beside the bed to awake her, but when she approached her face, she smelled the wine odor, for that she stopped try to awake her!, she looked to her aunt a reproof looking and urged her mother to leave the room, alleged to her mother that she is fine, needs some rest.

Sozan feigned that she believed her daughter so she left the room but she stilled behind the door to listen, she wants know what happened exactly.

After Sozan left Salma looked tigerish looking to Maria and told her with sharp voice:

- What do you did for her?.

Maria with calm voice:

- Nothing .. she drank some wine!.

Azza with low voice:

- I am .. ok .. Salma! .. just I sense some vertigo .. I am ok ..

Salma sat beside her on the bed held her hands asking:

- What are you doing here?, and where did you found the wine?.

Azza body shook laughed replied with English to let Maria know with sarcastic voice:

- I determined to test every thing in this stupid life, Maria helped me tested her wine today, and I will tested her too!.

When she said that Maria threw her by cushion cursed her with laughing, Salma slapped her cheek too:

- Ooh Salma .. Your aunt has a friend has a sweet cock!.

The two girls continued slapped Azza by cushions while Azza balled her body on the bed laughing try to save her body by her arms, Salma screamed with laugh for Azza and Salma:

- You are crazies! .. where you found this stupid guy?.. you will bring the problems for us!.

And she turned her face to her aunt saying her with warning voice:

- You are the responsible of all what happened!.

Maria replied with afraid voice:

- What I did? .. she is not a child!.. she is an adult! .. what I can did for her .. she want drinks wine!.

Salma stopped slapping Azza and replied her aunt:

- You brought the wine to the house and your stupid guy .. and you know that Azza is a reckless girl .. so you ought to stopped her .. but you are a reckless girl too!.

And with serious voice asked her aunt:

- I want ask you a question .. how you could brought a wine to a Muslims home .. where you knew that is forbidden for them? .. do you know that this is the first time wine or any other intoxicating thing entered into this house at all! .. this house chaste .. everybody in this home as an angel, pure, honest .. after your coming you opened all evil doors, we loved you .. but you exploited our love, our home, our family for your selfish and suspicious affairs .. I am sorry that you are my aunt.

She said that and left the room closing the door with force where she found her mother Sozan behind the door listened to all what happen in the room, she did not paid attention to her, she continued walking to her room with emotion.

Fatma searched for some thing needs in Azza room where found the Arabic copy of Gospel in her table roll when she was stood looking in the book Faris been in the door, he looked what his mother was examining, he entered the room and took the book from her hands, He amazed as his mother.

Maria prepared a strong black coffee for Azza and made many things for her to drive out the drunk from her mind, after few time Azza became well to walk to her house, when she was readied she left walking back to her house, while Maria stayed in her home in bad mood.

In the night where Mahmoud checked his home cameras memory he saw Mr. Shome arrived and depart and some of the Salon talking heard by a camera was been near the Salon out side window, he called Sozan to hear what happened, Sozan be shamed when she listened the shameless talking been in her salon, Mahmoud be nervous too, he did not believed his ears, Sozan did not found any excuses for her sister doing, so she cried as baby.

Mahmoud screamed her with thunder voice:
- Sozan .. make a salvation .. Your sister became a problem for us .. never I can accepted an unknown man been in our home .. I can not be patience anymore .. I am sorry Souzan she must be back to Milan .. I will cancelled her visa! .. and Salma have to cancel her friendship with Azza. She is not a good girl as what we think .. You must do the right .. I have no time for wrongs.

He said that to his cried wife while he continued his checked where he noted an unknown blue car carried two persons stopped in them home front, where them attention for the house, and other white car turned around his house way many times as spied about his home, wants know what happen inside while

Mr. Shome in the house and it followed his car when he departed, and saw the other blue car followed them too, and other unknown man passed the way walking many time around the house stopped from time to time beside the salon window listening.

Mahmoud asked his wife to see too, Sozan scared, she did not thought that her family was in serious trouble, many people followed them movements for unknown purposes.

Mahmoud felt the danger been near his family, he guessed that her relative suspicious behavior was the main cause of all this movement around his house, he don't know her relations facts and her purposes which made them in the light circle, as mice rounded with cats!, he concluded that many parts watching her and her friend, he don't know the reasons of each part, but they are really following her for some bad reasons, his mind on the point of explodes, but he did not found the way, Souzan look to him with sorry eyes, she wants continues her past easy life before her sister coming, without problems, but they became in blocked way.

Mahmoud took the phone and called his shop assistant to does not wait him tomorrow because he will be out, and called a beach hotel booking four rooms for two weeks from tomorrow for six people, and he ordered Sozan to make the family ready to leave tomorrow morning to the beach to spend some summer time on the beach to change them moods and with other point to take away Maria from the house till to her depart, Sozan agreed her husband for his quick performances, she thought too is that is the shortcut way to cut every new bad happens and save the family far of any followings from each one, she pleased for his idea, she kissed him thanking for his support and left out the room to inform all the family for them decision.

When Sozan entered Maria is room to inform her about them tomorrow trip decision found her in phone connection with Mss. Bella who informed her to go tomorrow to certain place in Tripoli to meet the Italian religious who will give her any helps need, Maria wrote the address and the phone number in a paper, Sozan heard some of the conversation end but she did not commented, Sozan informed her about tomorrow morning summer trip, Maria asked her to stay in home, but Sozan ordered her to be ready in the morning to combine the family, while Maria screamed rejecting her ordered Sozan left the room closing the door strongly.

The two boys surprised for them parent decision but they agreed, Salma guessed the purpose of her parent, she guessed that her father knew what happened today through his absented and he decided to do a safe performance against her aunt reckless behavior.

In midnight when Bera family on them beds and the house lights of Maria took all of them luggage in bags and let the house where Mohammed the taxi driver waiting her and carried her to the Italian person who promised her to Wait for her on the front of Mahari Hotel in his car, Mohammed carried her to her friend who put her luggage in the back of his car and left together.

In the morning at the breakfast while all the family carried them bags down, Sozan discovered that her sister was gone with all her luggage, her room was empty!, Sozan sat on the and step on the stairs and cried as a baby, slapping her face!.

Sozan asked Mahmoud to go to the police, she is under them responsibility, Police must know the circumstances of her gone to be the beginning of her visa cancellation, Mahmoud hesitated in beginning but he did not found any other way, for that he combined his sons and drove the car to the police station, where they gave an official statement content information about her and the date and time of her gone, two police men came to Mahmoud home examined her room and completed talking with Salma and Sozan, and took one of her big pictures!.

Mahmoud cancelled them summer trip, all the family was been sad, Salma cursed her aunt by screamed voice as crazy many times.

Mahmoud sent Sozan to search her in Barnouss house where she was not there, all quarter heard about her gone story, she made Mahmoud family conduct on any tongue, an occasion for joking, Sami and Faris and many other friends heard the news so they came to be with the family sons in the salon, some of neighbors been with Mahmoud in the front of house and the females with Sozan and Salma in the house hall, the situation was as status of death.

After few hours a police car carried two police men came with good news, that Maria is in safe but she is under arrest in Tripoli center police station with someone Italian too who they carried some forbidden and un-permitted things.

Sozan refused Mahmoud request to accompany him to visit her sister in the rest, for that Mahmoud combined with Salma to go with him to the police station, the investigator refused them asking to visit or see her, but he informed them that she was with an Italian man in suspicious status, where they were in a car in dark corner in marginal way and the driver who arrested with her run away when the police asked him for his documents!, they carried a bottle of wine which forbidden and some of Arabic gospel, but the Italian car has many unknown written papers and photos, and some gun bullets!, they are in bad legal status, he advised Mahmoud to get a lawyer for her.

When Mahmoud returned with his daughter to them home found an other bad news that a police car carried one driver man and two police women caught Azza and all females Barnous family too, Faris and his mother Fatma were been in edge of break-down.

Sozan some time cry, other time apologize to her neighbors, Salma tried to calm-down her mother, all females neighbors were in the home them eyes filled tears regretted for Mahmoud family bad situation become.

Maria confessed to the investigators for every what she did in Libya since her arrived up to her arrested, she was too scared, her false previous information about Muslims made her in the end point of scare, this is the first time she find herself face to face with the law severity, no friends, no family, no one can forgive her or overlook for one doing she did!, she *cried as never did before at the mercy of the investigators different questions.*

Mahmoud called a lawyer to take up the case of her and his neighbors females, he excepted the Italian man who did not knows, while most of the quarter talking about what happen, it was a big honor repute trouble.

Maria obscure doings disappointed Bera family even her sister and all around people, who welcomed and entertained her as them lost sister be back or arrived after long time.

Mahmoud family knows that what was happened today will be in the community memory for long time, people do not forget easy like this social news, Maria was done will be in people memory for long future time, maybe generation after generation, shame will be forever, for that people do not capable to do wrong or shame doings.

In quarter cafeteria some people exchanging information about Maria and some their women neighbors case, someone thinks that is a spying net, other one thinks is a Christ preaching net, some of them think is a prostitution case, others guessed that is a mixed matters case, all of them regretted for Mss. Azza that she has a good memoir in the quarter, the quarter were worried trying to hunt a new news.

Faris and his mother Fatma and Mahmoud family in the end of collapse!, they were together in Bera house silenced hearing Mahmoud phone talking with the lawyer and some other friends try to fix the problem by explaining the reality of his relative behavior, he needs their support, the case was under the security parts who do not share their inquiries with the police or anybody.

Maria crashed, in spite of that she told the full true to the investigators but they did not believed her, they need more information, they asked her some questions about some events and people who did not knows, they showed her some pictures of people to know them, but she did not, she did not know that the security agents want know everything about everything and do not care about her status, always has doubts about everybody, that is their job, (the doubt leads to fact) is their logo, they thought that when she confessed about something to hide other things, she was pure without any civil law fighting experience, this status carried a problems for all of her around friends who made or did unwanted doing or be out of the local law.

Azza disavowed her drunk in Mahmoud home!, and her receiving a copy of Gospel!, or her going to the Church!, but the police faced her with Maria who confirmed her talking on Azza face, but Azza insisted on her talking too, The Barnouss females had done like Azza doing, the security agencies made a pressure on Azza and Barnouss but their disavowing made them in good position in comparison with Maria who led herself down when confessed that she received the two wine bottles from Mr. Shome who became a part in the case, in charge of forbidden things alternation, also he became under the agents molars, Maria enlarged her case to seem as a plot.

Maria had sat in her dungeon crying, time to time the security agents calling her asking for something here or there while Maria answering them frankly, she thought that her frankly talking will be respected by them, but she was wrong, the facing with Azza and Barnous females and their denying harmed her feeling deeply, she thought that they had disowned her friendship!, she did not knew that they did that to do not be under law asking, and they don't want be a witness against her or against themselves, and them done lightened the police proofs heaviness for her.

The Italian who arrested with Maria in the car, The Italian helper, named in his official documents Signor Gabriel Polanski. who was an agent with Italy secret intelligence too, refused exchange any talking with the police, or the Libyan security agencies except his name, his work, but he denied Maria talking, he assured for the police that he did know Maria before, he found her in the hotel front searching for empty room, and because she was an Italian citizen too he decided helps her to find a room in other hotel, but he stayed with her in dark road to talk with her, and he assured that everything in the car is for Maria who brought its with her luggage, in facing with Maria he disowned Maria talking, and damned her where made Maria fainted.

Mr. Shome also he denied knowing with Maria and refused all her talking, but when the police inspected his house and office found many alcohol bottles boxes, and some drug that made him under the law inquiring, also Maria description for his office made him in law weak position.

The police put aside Mahmoud Family because they informed their police station about Maria suddenly absent, and on base of Maria informing to the security that Mahmoud family did not allowed her actions, and their good family reputation, but they inspected the houses of Barnous and Azza families, they found some alcohol and drug in Barnouss house but they found nothing forbidden in Azza home.

All the police and security agents inquiries was secret in the beginning, none knew what they are doing or what is the details of their inquiring.
Mr. Mahmoud has unlicensed gun graved it in his garden, all who was knew or met Maria been scared searching his own for any thing unwanted or forbidden, took care for police searching, some of them left their homes with their families to stay temporary with their relatives who were in other far place.

Maria coming was misfortune coming for Mahmoud family and all their neighbors and friends by all measurements.

After one week the situation came down, the police allowed visiting to Azza and Barnouss but they interdicted Maria and her two strangers friends visit, Shome and Gabriel who requested lawyers for them cases, but no one visited them, people thought that is a police trick to know their hidden friends, except Azza who visited by her mother Fatma and brother Faris.

Police searched for Mr. Barnous to arrest him in charge of alcohol and drug possessing but he was going, so the police waxed their home.

———

(9)
Battles in darkness

Through this quick events, Tripoli were in political secret civil disobedience, the two Libya neighbors Tunisia and Egypt peoples made civil revolutions against their dictator regimes, the Libyans also want do as their neighbors but their head of the dictator regime was been famous of bloody man, kills everybody against him, do not care about human rights or human global law, he governed Libya by steel hands, but the Libyans patience ended, they decided facing his regime with peace or force, they fed up of him, therefore most of the Libyans civil and uncivil forces got the chance to make him down.

The Libyans through some internet sites exchange the leaked news about what is happening in Libya which been hid by the regime, so the quarter families exchanging the last news about the regime and what they were doing in secret, The Libyan TV channels and all other media tools was under regime control, could not say single word out of orders, the Libyan regime as all dictators worldwide do not bear any criticism, if anybody has the enough courage to critique Algaddafi or his band, the regime heads, so he will be in dead Libyans list as soon as possible, therefore the death list is too long, contains thousands of good Libyans, who were asked for democracy, freedom, justice, the internet communication opened new large door for people to know the regime events as possible, which made a headache to the regime, who wants everything under his control.

Libyan regime took care for any event and explained it as a part of a general plan against them, even the normal crimes looked it as a political events, in short, the general situation of Tripoli was dangerous and unassuring, in bad luck the case of Maria been in this un-normal condition which exceeded the damage of all her case people.

Mahmoud as many Libyans closed his food shop and sat in home got ready for any surprises, his daughter Salma and his wife Sozan made themselves ready for arrest in any time!, all of the family was afraid and worry, Mahmoud listening to the radio and TV news of every channels wants know what is happening, collisions between Libyans and their regime force in everywhere, regime kills people in the streets on cameras faces, the Libyan young-men fight with the regime by everything, write phrases against the regime in every walls, break any regime statue and wipe any regime names or logo, make fire in tires in the streets and stones, , police inspect the cars and people and arrest everybody has any doubtful status.

Italy like some Europe countries condemned the Libyan dictator regime doing against the Libyans civil people, and his careless about the global human rights, where he kills civilian people in the streets without any trials, using the full force against civilians.

Mahmoud and his family surprised and shocked when the Libyan TV told in news that the Libyan police arrested an Italian spy net and showed the photos of Maria and her Italian friends, without any more details, Mahmoud thought surely that the Libyan regime made Maria case as a political case, to press on Italy politic because their condemning against him!, and to adulate the Libyans to hate Italy and the other European countries who said (No) for the dictator regime, Mahmoud knew that their regime is a criminal regime could do everything to get his bad goals, but the Libyans was too clever, they knew the regime lies traps before, for that they don't believe the regime even if they said the true!.

Salma and Sozan cried on Mahmoud chest as never done before, while Mahmoud wipes his eyes tears silently.

The quarter young-men like all Libyan young-men hate the dictator regime of their country Libya, they had done activity in their quarter in great union, they stood by on the ways in groups looking for every new, they closed the ways which lead to the quarter by heavy stones and some garbage, drove away the police out of the quarter, they incinerated their station and cars, and wrote phrases against the dictator regime on the quarter walls, the government power became out of the quarter like many places in Libya in that time, The Libyans showed the world a high courage which forced the world to respect them and hurried the countries for help, which made the dictator regime in Libya on the end step of fall.

Weeks next, the events became more than dangerous, the regime failed to surround the crisis, all the world condemned them bad doing against their people, the regime became lonely as Satan arranging plots for everybody, and kill every one stood in his way.

That Tripoli perfect life had gone, now you can see destruction and smoke everywhere, bloods on the blocked streets, people became crazy, don't care for the cost of heir freedom, and the regime became crazy too because they made all their criminal effort but their status returning backward every moment, all the world be against them, the united nation released an order and warning to Libya regime to stop their criminal doing, regime was fighting for their stay, Libyans was fighting for their liberty, both of them insist on victory, the force difference was too large, but the people courage lessened the distance.

The extremes Muslims parties fought the dictator regime with courage unparallel, in Benghazi the second capital of Libya and many east Libya cities people broke in many military camps and seized many weapons, they started armed fights, they began the Libya liberty war, so the regime air force became fire any people crowd in any places in Libya, it was a really war, the regime became an enemy of their citizens, USA and Europe encouraged the Libyans to go ahead against Algaddafi regime, people became crazy, the kill been everywhere, no one of every party wants do one step back.

The Libyans guessed that this is the last chance of them to break their slavery bonds, they resolved that there is no patience any more, death or victory, no other way!, the dictator regime showed them their dark face, that face which used all their past efforts to be hidden, alleged many honor slogans and liberty principles but every their promises was lies, just lies, every day were forwarding to be bad more that the day before, Libyans promised themselves to do not believe them any more, and will break down the liar dictator regime today not tomorrow!.

The Libyan civil war enlarged to be in most Libya, Algaddafi regime lost many cities and villages which been became under the revolutionaries government completely, revolutionaries became in the way to The country capital day after day, UN and liberalism world gave the air force support to the revolutionaries which froze the regime air force, that made a large space to the revolutionaries to go ahead to the west where Tripoli, for that the security in Tripoli and many cities and villages in the west and south which was under Algaddafi regime command became a large prison.

The civil war in the east reactions was tragic, Libyans in the west did not agreed Algaddafi regime killing people by arms, people were cried in the streets and threw the regime cars and agents by stones, they were happy when France air force broke down the regime military arms long queue, who were going to break in Benghazi, for first time the people happy for their national military broken!, a strange country force broke down their military force who was made to save their national land, but Algaddafi regime used it to kill their citizens.

The electricity power was lost for many hours per day, some times for some days, the fuel was been little in fuel stations, food became little in stores, the life became too hard.

Mahmoud with his close friends and their sons decided to be a part of this national revolution, they felt shame that they did not share their citizens efforts to drop this dictator regime, who lost them their freedom for long time.

After weeks later, in darkness attacks rotated against police and security stations and offices, short wars had been here and there, Mahmoud and his band had done many darkness attacks, his close neighbor friend Massoud killed in one of those darkness attacks, security spies had been everywhere try to know the enemies of the regime who attacked the government, all people were watching carefully every strangers and every movement in the streets around them, for that Massoud was graved in secret silently, his family was brave to accept that, they considered his death was martyr for Libya liberty, Mahmoud and his band promised his brave family to do not forget him forever.

Mahmoud band decided to attack the prison where Maria and her friends arrested, Faris The brother of Azza and Fathi the Barnous family head decided to share in the attack to free their relatives and all who was in the prison, for that most of the band had been around the prison to list every information to make the attack plan.

The pre-information insured that Maria and her friends had been still in the same prison, and there were many other Libyans arrested too in cases of against the regime and other small criminal cases, Ali in case of he was a civil engineer made a plan for the prison, and Bechir the electrical engineer made a plan to cut the prison interior electricity.

After all Pre-information completed the band made a meeting to discussing the plan, Mahmoud warned the band that the police will attack his home after the operation done because of Maria and Azza and Barnouss homes for the possibility that they were the attackers, therefore the plan must be enlarge to cover the regime possibility reaction, Said has a far small farm has a small house can be suitable residence for Maria and her two arrested friends, the band decided to supply the farm house with food and water and every important materials for long time residence for seven arrested before the operation start, to separate the farm and its house far of any outside movements for food or any other needs, and the two guards which must be not parts of the arrested family who will be under security spy watching!, so the farm car will carried the arrested from the prison to the farm directly in darkness follows by two arm cars for the way arresters safe until the farm near and the cars must be come back.

The plan ordered too, that they specialized an old far deserted house for the other unknown arresters to complete their sleep far of the regime eyes to their awake and then every body will take his way to his home with himself, that is the full help that can be done for them.

The plan contains some pre-action movement, that the arrested family parts must visit the quarter cafeteria the spies place lonely to drink coffee and play cards with others and to hear the spies some talks knowing as an agreeing for the regime actions, some of the band members will be in shifts around the prison to know any new information can changes their plan before the attack appointment, because the prison has many guards, who were about fifty soldiers, the band agreed to Saleh to seek help of other ten people to attack the prison with them under them order, that the total of the men who will attack the prison be about thirty men with their cars and guns, the plan contains many clever details, even they specialized members to carry everybody will damage through the fight to the secret clinic which done specially to this attack operation secretly, they covered all the ways which be used in withdrawal and will be close after the attack members run back, every body knew his act very well and what he must do after attack too, and for the next few days for his safe, the band made a secret clinic has two surgeons and some assistants ladies supplied with many surgery materials and needs.

The plan Including to specialize two members to make a friendship with the small restaurant near the prison people, the restaurant was the food supplier of the prison people, guards and arresters, every lunch time the restaurant sent a quantity order from eighty to one hundred and ten different lunches.

The two band members made a friendship with the restaurant workers through three days, one of the two band members was accepted to work with them as a carrying worker to carry the food to the prison and bring back the plates after lunch finish, he was able to confirm all the information and affirms the jails of Maria and her friends places, guards accepted him as a trusted person who works with the restaurant teem, the plan contains to put anesthetic in the prison food will be active at three hours in certain appointment.

After one week when everything had been done, in the darkness the attack had been done too, in the certain time the band member who was the restaurant carrying worker who put the anesthetic in the prison food made a call that every body in the prison was in deep sleep except about ten guards who he knows them places, every arrested became out of the prison without single gunshot after twenty one minutes.

About ten guards who did not eat their lunches surrendered silently under the band surprise who were arrested them in one of an empty jail without their mobiles or every connection tools, the band black veils seemed them as a terrorists which crept into the soldiers hearts a crazy fright, the other guards and most of the arresters had been in deep sleeping, Maria and her friends were sleepers too, so the band found a problem to take out the free sleepers to the cars.

The attack operation was quickly and silently, after one hour more every band members became in their homes except the restaurant worker and his partner was the new guards of the farm house where Maria and her friends new residence to guarding and to hiding themselves in same time, because they were known to the regime agents.

Every thing done as the plan orders as a professional soft job, after about two hours the local TV published the photos of the freed arresters who considered them spies to foreign intelligences, traitors and enemies to Libya, and added that there is a high *trained commandos of a foreign intelligence freed the prisoners and carried them to unknown direction.*

All the band members had been glad, their good plan seemed them as a trained commandos of intelligences , which will make any accusation far of them, they thanked Allah deeply, but all of them must follow the plan orders for the next days, all the band members who shared to the attack operation amazed that their doing was perfect without single gunshot, everyone of them congratulated his self and thanked Allah that no one wounded, they done the attack as magic done, they were too lucky in this time.

Maria and her friends surprised when they found themselves in a special closed house, every body in single closed room, but they put Azza and Barnous three females in one room together because the house has just four rooms, the guards covered them faces by veils, they seemed as a terrorists, the plan ordered that the guards to not exchange any conversation with the free prisoners, they must treat them as a strangers, in the beginning the prisoners tried to protest claiming to talk with the official of the kidnappers, but the two clever guards threatened them by arms to be quiet.

The regime had not guessed that some civilian people can made like this professional attack plan, they ascribed the operation to foreign professional part who be able to practice this clever plan without any mistake in record time, therefore they put aside that the Libyan arresters relatives can do it anyway, so they concentrated them watching to the strangers sides or people.

For more misleading Mahmoud and Faris requested Algaddafi authorities for their relatives who had been in the prison under the government responsibility and have been kidnapping from the prison.

Fights became everywhere, Nato air force waging attacks everyday on Libya military forces, Libyans on the land using all them efforts to make the revolution successful, families graved their relatives silently with courage and honor, the regime be crazy, the world amazed for the Libyans courage and stubbornness.

In the streets people discussing every new news, religious people, liberalists, every political or culture directions be in one line, against the dictator regimes, looking for democracy future for them country, people talking about the prison attack operation, they denied Algaddafi TV talking, that the fugitives prisoners were against Libyans or Libya as a country, they guessed that if the regime TV said that, so the fugitives prisoners were against the dictatorial regime, so they are a part from the Libyans revolution, because the regime always describes the Libyans evolutionists as traitorous, agents for foreign sides.. est.

After few days Mahmoud team amazed when they saw in TV Libyan people carried the fugitives arresters photos as strivers for freedom and democracy against Algaddafi and his regime!, Maria and her two strangers friends and Azza and the three Barnous females were included with the photos which carried by the people in the large of Libya with enthusiastically words wrote on large sign-boards!, as a big freedom fighters against dictatorship.

When Mahmoud saw that Maria and her strangers friend became strivers in the Libyans view so he ordered his team or band to guard the church because he guessed that the regime will attack it in case of Maria informed them about her visiting to the church.

Mahmoud long view saved Mrs. Bobo and his church colleagues from the regime arresting, the regime in that night sent two cars to arrest them Indeed, but Mahmoud band and some of other people confronted them in short fight, which forced them to run away with some wounded!.

Faris the Brother of Azza and Ali harmed in church fight where they had sent to the secret clinic, Faris harm was an external hits, but Ali was in dangerous case.

Mahmoud Band emptied the church, Mahmoud distributed them in his neighbors houses as a guests to be far of the regime hands, who searching for any reason to catch any foreign people to bargain with their countries who had closed their embassies in Tripoli, cause of unsafe status who had been in Tripoli and because they took a negative stance with the dictator regime of Libya and they supported the revolutionists.

The revolutionists supported by Nato air force became near Tripoli the Stronghold of Algaddafi regime who be staggering, his grip became soft, just some thousands became around him, people blows from everywhere against every his movements, most of his agents fled to outside Libya by forger passports with a lot of the Libyans money.

Algaddafi and his regime popularized for many months on their media tools that Libya will be a split country if the Nato revolutionists (as what the regime nicknamed the Libyans revolutionists) will seize the country, because many parts was being through the revolutionists, many of them had been wanted from the global court for terrorism cases, many of them were in Afghanistan fought the freedom world forces, and the country will be under the authorize of the excessive Muslims, terrorists and thieves, many people believed them, they knew well that he was a killer and thief too, but the choice was between the bad and the very bad, people do not want divide their country to pieces or under different authorizes, but most of the people seek a good omen for their country, the choice was very difficult, many people were in unbalance case, many people sat in their homes put themselves aside, watching the events around them with worry and scare.

Many people were hesitated, they did not believed all what Algaddafi and his regime speech in their media, but they were scared for their country future, they don't want their country be under the authority of the excessive Muslims, they hated their old-fashioned regime in Afghanistan which showed their narrow-minded, and their hate to other people who did not similar for them.

Libya became a large university, all ideas was on the table, many people were talking, but many people were being quiet too, no one can knows the future, every talk was guesses, just guesses, encouraged by Nato and some of revolutionists media, who encouraged Libyans who were under Algaddafi regime cities to use their efforts with the revolutionists efforts to break down the dictatorial regime with force, promising Libyans to build a new democrat regime in Libya as one country, not as what Algaddafi regime saying in his media tools.

The old Libyans political parties who Algaddafi stopped their activities since long time renewed them selves and started them activities again with some shame, the old culture or political ideas been under study and conversation again too, every body became a new philosopher, but most of Libyans believed The Nato and UN media and their promises about the future of Libya, but only the future will show the facts, if that is really or no, if no, so the Libyans took the wrong way for their country future, often they will not can fix their mistake easily, and the chance to build a new democracy regime in their country will be lose.

Ali lost one of his legs, doctors can not gathering the bone pieces of one of his legs, therefore they amputated the leg from knee to do not poison his body, some people thought the farm house is one of Algaddafi regime intelligence secret places therefore they attacked it in the darkness where they fought with the two guards who asked them team or band members for help, Mahmoud sent five members included his two sons for the fighting, his close friend Bechir the farm owner and his young son Ali had been killed, but the band forced the attackers to run away, therefore

Mahmoud took the prisoners out to an other hidden place, it was a long bloody night.

Mahmoud did not cried when he received his son and his close friend bodies in the darkness, but he sat down beside the way looking to the stars of the sky silently, as he seek Allah mercy for his death friends and son, all his alive group rounded him, Mahmoud repeated Sura-Alfatiha and some other chapters of the Holy Koran and asking Allah to mercy them and all the revolution martyrs who gave their souls for Libya freedom!.

Souzan and Salma cried silently but they arose a brave behavior when they had met people who had come for consolation in secret.

After graving Mahmoud and all alive teem or band went together to the hidden house with Fatma the mother of Azza and Sozan to the hidden house where the arresters live, Maria and her friends had cried for long time, that they did not guessed that they were been out of the prison by them relatives and friends, Mahmoud apologized to Maria and her friend for them freeing postponement yet now, and them treating as strangers because of them safety, for that they delayed them freedom from time to time, but now the regime hands became broken and everything will be alright, Mr. Fathi get out his wife and his two daughters, Souzan took out her sister, and Fatma associated Azza to the car, while Saleh accompanied the two other Italians to be his guests to the time of the Italy embassy opening, it was a happy time for all the arresters in spite of the around dangerous in the darkness, nine cars run slowly without light in dark marginal ways

———

(10)
Reversely Scales

The debates about Libya future after Algaddafi gone was everywhere, as if the people want know or see the future, everybody even the revolutionists had been scared, they did not know the background culture of many parts who were being parts of the revolution, also Libyans look with doubt eyes to the west (USA and Europe), who has a high technology and high cunning and tricks too, through this subject oneself Masjed Imam invited the quarter people to a meeting in the Masjed to talk and exchange ideas.

In correct time The Masjed had been full, most quarter people were been there, even Maria and the two Italians and Mr. Bobo and his Christians Church colleagues who were been a guests with some quarter families, Masjed Imam sat women in side and men in other side in the Masjed hall, in same time he stood some young men been out the Masjed with guns for guarding.

The Masjed Imam did not ascended (Menbar) - a high place has some stairs in front of the hall-, but he sat down on a chair to see everybody facing him, Imam saluted people and thanked them for coming and asked people to talk frankly without extend to give chance for all to talk, and he saluted Mr. Bobo and every Christians who be in this meeting, and ordered people who has been speaking Italian language to translate the talking to them, for that Sozan moved to sat beside

Maria and someone moved to sat between the two Italians to translate for them.

The first talker said:

- Mr. Imam, Brothers and Sisters, Libya will be in unknown condition, a new unknown status, there is many powers been on Tripoli door, will be here in few days when we help them, the UN did nor agreed the revolution in really without including the country capital, the war did not get victory where the country capital not be under the attackers authorize, therefore we must know our way through this anarchy, we fought Algaddafi and his bands for many months, and many of us had been killed in this stupid war and many people had been wounded, we waded into the wars without any previous training, but I think we did not so bad if we did not been better than the professionals, so we must do not give our future which paid a souls of our favorite people for it to an unknown people maybe they are more than Algaddafi criminals and dictators, or to excessive Muslims powers who will change our life by the name of Allah to dark future ..

Other one have a long black beard stood up and interrupted him saying:

- What do you mean that the excessive Muslims power will ...

Imam signed to the last talker to sit down saying:

- sit down please .. let him complete his talking!

The first talker completed:

- Like this sample as what I want have to warning people, before few minutes apposite Masjed before our entering this man was criticized our Imam for his

invitation to women to be in this meeting and he refused entering Christians to the Masjed, and now he want stop everybody talk to say the reality .. what we can do with like these people in the future?, these people knew the religion through narrow mind, women were in every Masjed, every market and in every Muslims wars beside men in the time of the prophet Mohammed to now, the Libyan females, ladies and Misses were with us in this war, Omar and many old Muslims were been praying in Christians churches, there is no problem, but these people want make problems in any life movements .. our future will be not good as what we hope if like these people govern us .. Salamo Alaikom.

The second man asked Imam to talk, said:
- We are not mindless, or we knew the Islam through a narrow view points as what the first talker said but we ..

The Imam interrupted him again saying:
- Please .. we are here talking about the Libya future, we not to discuss other view points .. enter our subject directly!.

The man continued:
- Ok .. People scared or worried for the Muslims authority, Muslims do not the people enemies, they are Libyans too ..

Some one from the rear said with high voice:
- Algaddafi was a Libyan too!.

The Man re completed his talk looking to the voice source:

- Yes brother .. he was a Libyan but he did not fear in Allah, he can do what he could do, always he had killed most of the educated civilian Libyans in jails ..

Imam re interrupted him again saying:

- Please sir .. We are not here to discuss Algaddafi crimes .. please talk in our subject.

- OK .. Imam .. I want people know that there is no reason to take a negative stand against Muslims authority!, everyone will care Libya and its citizens using the full of his effort to be in the front line of the respected nations.

Other one took talking:

- I am sorry that there is some Libyans became agents of global terrorism organizations, who has a lot of money where explained the simply Islam as what they wished, Libyans did not wish extremism in any subjects of our life sides, in fact that we are fear and worry about out future life, our sons life, who lost their souls for good future for their country and citizens, for freedom, democracy, justice, we are not brokers, we paid the freedom cost, so we must take care, our arms must be with us, in our hands, to use it when there is no other way to fix mistakes or correct authority direction, If Muslims or any national parties want be our new governors, the single way for them to do that is the election boxes way, no one will impose his ideas with force, we will continue our people struggle who had been died or still alive, we will not forget our people who died for us, and we will not sell them blood, or their sacrifice, we will react with our citizens, everybody can do everything without force

using, and we must be here as a freedom guards .. thank you .. Salamo Alaikom.

Mahmoud took talking said:
- Brothers, we are in new liberal condition, we were in curb status since long time, forty years we have been talking carefully, any Gaddafi spy can makes a report will lead you to death, but in spite of them we continued our life in our country because we have not other country to live in it, we worry about our future, that is true, but we must not let our worry lead us to be back, we chose our way, against injustice, dictatorship, decay, for our country future, so we must continue our way, we have worry but we have hope too, we trust in our god Allah that he will helps us to be in good and fine.

When Mahmoud finished his talk, Mr. Bobo asked requesting talk, Imam sign to him to talk:
- Firstly, I am too happy to be among my Muslims friends and brothers in their Masjed where they worship Allah our god, We felt ashamed that some people killed for our safe, who we were not been in your religion, and we are you guests, you opened your houses and your hearts for us, you killed yourselves to safe us, talking or any other thing do not give you your rights, you are a great brave Muslims .. Thank you Mr. Mahmoud for you perfect leadership, thank you Mr. Imam to let me feel that I and my Christians colleagues part of your human care can fight for their safe and freedom, thank you our family hosts who considered us as their family members, we will not forget what you did for us .. if you did not helped us we

had been dead or in dark places under torture for crimes we did not done!.

When Mr. Bobo said those words the cry stopped him to complete, many men around him stood up hugged him, try with him to be calm, dried his teardrops, some of them brought to him some water.

Imam welcomed the Christians and asked them to come for him for any question or need, and after few other talks he ended the meeting, hoped for all good times, so everybody went back to his home silently.

Every arrested been in his family home spend his time watching TV or using internet if the electricity is connected, which connects for few hours daily, water is cut some times too, Azza lost her smile, Faris with some neighbors young men sit in the front garden of Mahmoud family with their arms, the front garden became as a station for the band or team, using internet connections link with other Libyans exchange news and every new movements, and to guard Mahmoud and his family because he is as the commander of the band, Mourad the old son of Mahmoud became the post officer of the team.

Mahmoud spend his most time in his room, prays or reading Koran or watching TV news, using internet to know the last news and exchange ideas with other revolutionists in the large of Libya and make internet calls for revolution job, all quarter people coming to him for any reason, and to consult him for every thing, and they obeying him to do everything with pleasure, he became as a public leader, all the quarter armed men became in his order, therefore he was a commander of about three hundred armed men, *controlled all the quarter, no one can go out or enter the quarter for any reason without his order, so his house became as a head control department, the quarter people admired for him as a simple clever honest leader, he became known in most of Libya, his prison attack perfect plan made him in the first class of the revolution leaders, for that the quarter became as his own soldiers practice his talk without discussing.*

Maria in her old room crying the majority of time, her arrested and all other next events showed her how she was far of the right, her sister son and many others died for her safety, to be free, if Mahmoud and his friends and sons did not attacked the prison and carried her out of the hell, so she had been died or what that Satan regime will do with her, she remembered her sister died son, his smile, his beauty and his honest doing, now he is under earth, his soul faraway, she did not thought that Muslims like every good people, Arabs is as any people has good and has bad, but the good is more than the bad, this simple words many people tried to let her hear it, but she was deafen, she pressed her sister family in blood position, never be forget.

She left a paradise house in darkness as a thief without saying good bye, for what?, to throw her self in spy hold, as a blind person, she was not a spy, she came for her sister and to let people know Christ, but she found Muslims know Christ more that she, in jail Muslims gave her in secret their food and medications to be alive and encouraged her to withstand, they told her to do not say any names or events, but she was crazy that she brought every his knows to prison as a fool girl, she brought damage for every body and killed her sister son, nobody scolded her, even her sister family, her sister Sozan became the good example for the really women.

Far of six housed after Mahmoud is house Mr. Polanski Gabriel as what he named himself was a guest of Mr. Ali is family, who his leg had been cut, he asked Mr. Ali to help him to visit her house, he needs a car and some armed men to go with him because his house is in the west side of Tripoli and can not went through the city lonely without covering, Ali told him that his going outside the quarter is too dangerous, but for insure he sent his son to inform Mahmoud about his guest request, Mahmoud replied Ali his refusing in cause of that there is many fights been out the quarter, all ways had been closed, Ali informed his guest for Mahmoud order, and warned him that Mahmoud is ordered him to stay calm in the house for his safety.

Mr. Bobo came to Mahmoud is house with Mr. Shome who asked him to go with him to Mahmoud for the same reason, Mahmoud informed Mr. Shome too as what he said to Mr. Gabriel, he ordered him too to stay in home under them guarding because he can not save his life outside the quarter.

Barnouss sat in their house silently, their house door been closed all the time, which was been opening all the time, they felt ashamed for their arrest case, their past high noise laughing along the quarter streets had been gone, no pleasure requested people knock their house door be anymore, for the first time felt worry and isolation, their arrest gave them a new experience, it was hard days difficult to be forget, the life showed them its hard face.

People in the quarter became as one family, sharing food, water, materials, everything, Mahmoud and many traders in the quarter supplied people for everything needs for free, some communication technicians changed some radios to wireless free frequency receivers which made them able to hear every words of the regime wireless communications, others attacked the regime internet websites which try to mislead Libyans about the facts, Nato air force attacks been along the time, every Tripoli quarters been as a closed parts, regime has just the city center, the Tripoli around became out of their control, people operated electrical generators everywhere, bombs sounds hear in every times, Mahmoud ordered his people to save food, water, medicines and every important materials in the their house underground floors, and his soldiers to be separately, every two, three people together, some bombs rockets fallen on some houses by mistake killed one child and harmed some others, Mahmoud followed by all the quarter families raised the old Libya flag on their houses, and on armed men crowds, as a signals to Nato air force pilots, that they are revolutionists, Mahmoud called Nato attacks operation room through the internet and gave them some information about their location and many more information about the status on the ground.

Mr. Gabriel did not want be under the quarter order, for some reason he wants go out from the quarter urgently, so in dawn early he stole Ali is gun and his car keys and sneak out the home, he removed away the car number boards and run away, he informed the quarter portal guards who knew him that he go out for some reason under Mahmoud order, so they allowed his going out with warning that he will be in actual dangerous outside the quarter, but he insisted on them, in that time Ali detected the stealing of his gun and car, Ali called the gate guards who informed him that Mr. Gabriel passed the gate to outside the quarter, Ali Informed Mahmoud who asked him to have patience, and sent to him an other gun, Mahmoud informed Mr. Bobo about what Mr. Gabriel done in darkness, for any future reason, the quarter heard what happened, but there is nothing to do.

After few days Mahmoud received the corpse of Mr. Gabriel who killed in his stolen car because he opened fire to some revolutionists who ordered him to stop, in the west of Tripoli, but because they saw his photo in TV, they considered him as a revolution helper, so from hands to hands secretly they carried his body to Mahmoud quarter with his stolen car and gun too, Mahmoud asked Mr. Bobo to pray for his soul as a Christian and put the corpse in well-knit plastic and put the bag in freezer connected with generator, all the quarter people been sorry for his death.

The events continued quickly, Ramadan (the yearly Muslims fasting month) had been came, the other cities like Musrata, Benghazi, Zouara, who were near the sea and got their freedom, out of Algaddafi regime authority received many food and human needs from the Arabs and Muslims counties who stood up to help the Libyans revolution, until many desert villages an cities like Sebha, and many of the west

Libya mountain villages, but Tripoli and some other places who were under the dictatorial regime, the people supplied by themselves, so the food, medications and fuel been too short, the electricity times been too short, the internet connection been closed too.

The regime used all their force to re-back his authorial on all Tripoli around quarters but they failed, many fights been far of the city center, always people seized many arms from the regime bands in any fight.

At twenty of Ramadan in darkness the east revolutionists entered to Tripoli center from the sea used light boats and guns, they began their attack from the interior of the regime fort aria directly, this clever directly attack unbalanced the regime control, they became operate the fight which been in his home, the people had been learned the regime a new war lesson, how they can fight and win, the fights continued three hard days, which forced Algaddafi and his band to runaway to Sirt village, his birthplace.

People chased Algaddafi and his bands to his birthplace and its nearly villages, Tripoli had been opened, embassies opened their doors again, the country will be in big public party, smiles been back again on Libyans lips.

Mahmoud handed the body of Mr. Gabriel to Italy embassy with report explained what happened with him and the condition of his death, and short condolence letter for his family, and informed them about Maria who lost her passport too, the Italian ambassador thanked Mahmoud and his band for their help, the quarter received some Italian agents who came and asked people about Mr. Gabriel death, and promised Maria to produce an other passport for her to leave Libya as her wish, Mr. Shome went to his home in safe had been thanked Mahmoud and the quarter families for their hospitality and care.

--- END ---

Author books صدر للمؤلف
****

1 دراسات Studies

1- الاستخبارات العسكرية ـ تطبيق إداري معاصر ـ (ج 1).
2- الاستخبارات العسكرية ـ عمليات الميدان - (ج 2).
3- (The Big Knot).
4- (العقدة الكبرى) – ترجمة لكتاب The Big Knot).
5- (حصافة 2013-2012) مجموعة مقالات حصافة.

2 روايــــات Novels

1- (صديقتي الفرنسية)(My French Girlfriend).
2- (عاد مع الريح) (Came back with wind).
3- (انتقام الأبرياء) (Innocents Revenge).
4- (That is what the stone said!).
5- (Runaway to The West).
6- (Born against Government).
7- (Bullet in Darkness).
8- (From notebook of Apostate).
9- (A Man from The Middle-East).
10- (On Europe Steps).
11- (A Story has a beginning).
12- (The Last Man).
13- (A Muslim In our house).